Happy Tailgating II!

Jaymee Ashley & Kelli Ashley

Kentucky TALEgating II

More Stories with Sauce

Kelli Oakley & Jayna Oakley

ACCLAIM PRESS
MORLEY, MISSOURI

AUTHOR'S ACKNOWLEDGEMENTS

Almost three years ago, we started collecting recipes, stories and photos from tailgaters across Kentucky. We never thought about where it might take us or how it might end. But 208 pages later, numerous festivals and book signings, more interviews, photos and an international award, we had no other choice but to complete Kentucky TALEgating II: More Stories with Sauce! As always, we thank our famililes for bearing with us on weekends and nights away, our friends and co-workers for listening to all our travels, tailgaters for letting us intrude on game day, and the many businesses, bookstores, gift and specialty shops who are carrying our first book. One person we, along with all the University of Kentucky RV Roadcats, also thank and will miss is Betty Browning, from Lancaster, Kentucky. During our first few visits to Commonwealth Stadium, Mrs. Browning ushered us in and out of everyone's "campsites" and told us "everything we needed to know about tailgating." Mrs. Browning passed away two seasons ago. Again, we thank all of you who have played a part in making our first book a success and giving us the motivation for doing book number two!

(Top left) Jayna Oakley, left, and Kelli Oakley take to the "road" in gathering recipes for the Kentucky TALEgating II: More Stories with Sauce cookbook. (Bottom left) Betty Browning, far right, will be missed by the Oakley authors. She spent time with Kelli and Jayna helping them gather recipes for their first cookbook. Mrs. Browning passed away a couple of football seasons ago. (Right) Kelli Oakley, left, and Jayna Oakley pose during a book signing at Joseph-Beth Booksellers in Lexington.

Peggy Cummins, Lawrenceburg, left, and Jackie Allen, Midway, throw bean bags during a corn hole game at a University of Kentucky football game.

ACCLAIM PRESS INC.
Your Next Great Book
P. O. Box 238
Morley MO 63767
(573) 472-9800
www.acclaimpress.com

All book-related correspondence should be addressed to:
Oakley Press
P. O. Box 911031
Lexington KY 40591
(859) 433-6459
(859) 494-1027
www.oakleypress.net
email: oakleys@oakleypress.net

Book Design:Ron Eifert
Cover Design: Eric Winke
Special Graphic Effects: Matthew Skaggs

Library of Congress Catalog No: 2007928969
ISBN: 0-9790025-8-3

Printed in the United States of America
First Printing, August, 2007
10 9 8 7 6 5 4 3 2 1

Additional copies may be purchased from Acclaim Press

This publication was produced using available information. The Publisher regrets it cannot assume responsibility for errors and omissions.

From page 1: Parrish House is filled with University of Louisville memorabilia and attracts many tailgaters for the university's home games.

TABLE OF CONTENTS

HAIL MARY'S...An Introduction to Talegating 8

PLAYBOOK...Play by Play of Tailgating 12

KICKOFFS...Chips, Dips & Other Starters 17

RUFFAGING THE KICKER...Salads-Hot &Cold 39

BOWL GAMES...Soups, Chilis & Stews 59

BUN WARMERS...Burgers, Hotdogs & Sandwiches 83

HEATING UP THE GRIDIRON...Steaks, Ribs & Other Main Dishes 91

OFF SIDES...Veggies, 'Taters & Other Side Dishes 119

HOW SWEET IT IS!...Cakes, Cookies & Other Sweet Treats 135

CHEER-LITERS...Punch, Mixers & Sippers 167

HASH MARKS...Measurements 179

THE GAME ROSTERS...The Game Chefs 181

INDEX 184

Parrish House shows Cardinal spirit

Al Parrish, retired general manager of Ford, got together with several of his friends about 10 years ago and bought an old building near Papa John's Stadium and renovated it for a place to tailgate during University of Louisville football games. Now, these 10 or so friends have turned into a 100 member and 200 guest party, compliments of two guest passes given to each member for all the home games. Parrish also invites another 100 or so guests from each opposing school on game day. One game, each year, Parrish rolls out the patriotic carpet for some special guests. On Dec. 2, 2006, he invited 1,000 soldiers from Ft. Knox to attend the game, eat pizza and enjoy pre-game festivities. Located inside the Parrish House is a wall each soldier signs his name to before leaving.

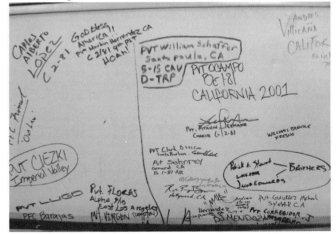

(Left) Soldiers from Ft. Knox line up to take their seats during a University of Louisville Cardinal football game in 2006. Al Parrish invites 1,000 troops every year. (Above) Before leaving for the game, soldiers leave a signed message on the walls of the Parrish House.

(Top left) The Parrish House is filled with University of Louisville memorabilia. (Bottom left) Parrish House runs its own concession stand at Papa John's Stadium. (Top right) Becky Brockway, who helps out in the Parrish House during game day, poses with Al Parrish. (Below right) Visitors to the Parrish House get into the spirit of the game with posters and memorabilia like the one below.

Hail Mary's...Season II

Kentucky TALEgating: Stories with Sauce brought the tales, photos and favorite foods of Kentucky's die-hard fans and their unpredictable weather, favorite teams and most memorable moments to life in more ways than we could've ever predicted!

Through a collection of recipes and photos, fans from different schools, of all ages, races, religions and backgrounds shared their stories of relationships built through bumper to bumper parking lots of smoking grills and stories! Many of the recipes collected for this edition have been passed down from generation to generation of tailgaters and football fans.

Any football fan who has braved the frigid temperatures and the thermometer-breaking heat waves knows that tailgating is an important part of any football game in Kentucky. From stoking the fires of their grills to keeping ice chests full of their favorite drinks and ales to the camaraderie of reuniting with friends to remember football days and seasons gone by...tailgating has truly become TALEgating to all these Kentucky fanatics!

For a few Saturdays in the fall, we talked to the football junkies, who have been eating, drinking, laughing, talking, singing, dancing and reminiscing about the games that were and predict the games that will be! Because of these tailgaters, Season II was a must! It's more of the same—dressing in favorite team colors, predicting the outcomes, meeting and talking with opposing school fan talegaters, posing for photos, getting mascots painted on your face, catching up with old friends, waiting in line for the port-a-potties, arguing with friends about the play that turned things around, planning road trips, playing corn hole games, praying, hoping it doesn't rain or snow or get too hot, looking for extra tickets, getting rid of tickets and saying, "I remember when..." and mostly hoping it doesn't have to end in November!

We hope you enjoy more of the same with Kentucky TALEgating II: More Stories with Sauce!

During a book signing in Georgetown, Kentucky, Jayna and Kelli Oakley met Sherri Beth McKee, wife of Scott County High School Cardinal football coach Jim McKee. Sherri Beth said she wanted to contribute recipes from the "Touchdown Club Tailgating Party" team. The club got together every week and shared food and recipes. Once some of the dishes became favorites, there were requests for recipes. As a result, the group put together a collection of Scott County Touchdown Club Friday Night Favorites. Jayna and Kelli would like to thank Sherri Beth for contributing these recipes and sharing them with everyone. Pictured is a Friday night Cardinal tailgate party.

Blackford Parks Cars on Saturdays; Prepares Healthy Dishes on His Off Days

Jim Blackford has been parking cars during the University of Kentucky games since 1969. When he's not in the parking lot, however, he spends time converting regular desserts to a lower sugar version for his daughter Ann, who underwent a kidney-pancreas transplant several years ago. Ann says his dishes are not only healthy but make a beautiful presentation as well. One of her favorite recipes is included in this book, "Jim's Fruity Angel-Food Trifle." Below left: Jim Blackford puts the finishing touches on his fruity angel-food trifle. Right, he poses with his daughter, Ann, and the finished dessert.

Oakley/Blackford Team Up for UK

Committee of 101 club members Jim Blackford of Nicholasville and Gene Oakley (father of author Jayna Oakley) of Lexington have been parking cars during University of Kentucky football games since 1968 and 1969, respectively. Each have parked cars at the University's old Stoll Field and Commonwealth Stadium. Below left: Jim Blackford, left, and Gene Oakley get ready to begin parking the hundreds of cars that begin hunting a space three hours before kickoff. Below right: Gene Oakley assisted Doug and Sharon Quinn, both of Lexington, in parking during the University of Kentucky/University of Georgia game in 2006.

Playbook...Play by Play of Tailgating

Getting ready for an upcoming season of football in Kentucky usually means realizing you have to pack several types of clothing for all of Kentucky's fickle weather. Once you have this gear packed, which may include raincoats, overcoats, extra socks and other apparel in your school colors, you can pretty much leave it in your vehicle for the remainder of the season or until you need to use it. Remember, just like the change of possessions in a game, so is Kentucky's unpredictable weather!

Now, it's time to begin planning your menu and make sure you do the prep work a day or two before the game. This is where you will want to remember to keep the menu simple so that you'll have time to enjoy old friends and tantalize new neighboring tailgaters. Bring food prepared and stored in disposable containers or bring food you can throw on a grill. For the "social tailgater," you can also stop on the way to the game and buy it ready to eat.

Whether you cook or bring food already prepared, make a list of the items you plan on taking including paper dinnerware, trash bags and damp towels. No matter how large your party of tailgaters, remember, too, you will be sharing with wanted and unwanted neighbors and new friends. So bring lots of everything!

If you plan on cooking, make sure you've filled your propane tanks or have brought plenty of charcoal,

lighter fluid and matches. No fire site is complete without tables and chairs. You will want to arrive at least three or four hours early to begin your whole cooking process, as well as finding a great parking space. If at all possible, park near a grassy spot or at the end of a parking row and by all means, near a port-a-potty.

Once your food is on the grill, you will want to spend some time getting out your school flags and decorating your site. If you have electricity, you will definitely want to fire up your boom box and play your school fight song as loud as you can or at least until your neighbors begin to complain. As you continue checking your grill, make sure you tune into your local pre-game show and begin making bets with the neighbors on the outcome of the game. If the game is on television, find a good outside location that you will be able to see the television, both in the sunlight and at night. If you have tickets on the 50-yard line, forget the television, radio and your friends and neighbors!

Some of the most important items not to be forgotten on any tailgate day is a cooler full of ice, bottle opener, first-aid kit, toilet paper, sun block, game tickets, parking pass, jumper cables, grill utensils, antacids, more ice, coffee for the next morning, hot sauce, comfortable shoes, friends and more ice!

Enjoy your tailgating season and the stories, great food and fun you will share with one another!

Whayne Supply Company enjoyed some pre-game festivities before the Wildcats took on the Georgia Bulldogs at Commonwealth Stadium in 2006. Visitors include, left to right, Monty Boyd (President), Andrew Boyd, Ben Phillips, David Hopekamp, Jan Hopekamp, Mary Fuson and David Fuson. The Whayne Supply group has been tailgating for 15 years.

TALEgating Fun and Games...

Cecil Jackson, left, closes his eyes during a test of gravity at one of the University of Kentucky football games. Jeanie Burgess, center, wearing white shirt and jeans, and Michele Ratliff place their hands above Jackson, seated. As more hands are added and rubbed together, Jackson's gravitational pull begins to elevate, right, and he is lifted by the force of gravity.

WKU Alums Enjoy Decade of TALEgating

Dave Gay (left) and Jason Clay Comb, WKU tailgaters

Dave Gay and Jason Clay Comb have tailgated at Western Kentucky University home games for the past 10 years. Both are WKU graduates, 1985 and 1995 respectively. Gay and Comb usually pack a grill and set up a tent to tailgate with 12 or so other friends and family during the Hilltoppers football season. Gay, from Peoria, IL, said that when he graduated in 1985, there was no tailgating and is pleased how many fans now tailgate. Gay, who played baseball for the Hilltoppers, also said the best part of tailgating is the camaraderie and everyone getting together, telling lies and watching the lies grow each year. Comb also said it doesn't pay to brag when you're a new tailgater. According to Comb, from Horse Cave, Kentucky, he traveled to Louisville "in a big ol' truck" for a game between the Cardinals and Hilltoppers. He left the windows down and the radio playing for several hours. When told he had better be careful because he would run the truck's battery down, Comb said he answered coolly that he had plenty of "time." However, Comb said his truck and crew was the last to leave the field because his battery was "deader than a doornail" and his truck had to be jumped. Everyone got a good laugh!

KICK-OFFS

Chips, Dips
& Other Starters

Tortilla Roll-ups

1 package (8-10) flour tortillas (large size)
8 ounces cream cheese
8 ounces sour cream
1 small can chopped green chilies
1 small can chopped black olives

Mix cream cheese and sour cream. Add chilies and olives. Spread over tortillas and roll up. Refrigerate overnight. Slice and serve with salsa.

Lee Clevenger
Lexington, Kentucky
Bryan Station High School Defender Fan

Mrs. Hilen's Chutney Cream Cheese Spread

8-ounce cream cheese, softened
½ jar Major Grey Mango Chutney
6 slices bacon, fried crisp
3 to 4 green onions

On a cake plate, spread cream cheese. Spread the chutney over the cream cheese. Crumble the bacon and place on top of the chutney. Chop green onion into small pieces and top the bacon with green onions. Spread bacon and green onions on top right before serving. If made ahead, be sure to refrigerate until time to serve. Serve with crackers.

Sandy Hilen
Lexington, Kentucky
University of Kentucky Wildcat Fan

Goal Post Crunch

6 cups (9 ounces) mini pretzels
6 cups Chex or Crispix cereal
1 cup pecans
½ cup butter or margarine
1 cup brown sugar, packed
¼ cup light corn syrup
1 teaspoon vanilla
½ teaspoon soda

Combine pretzels, cereal, and nuts and set aside. In 2-quart glass bowl, melt butter, then add brown sugar and corn syrup and mix. Microwave brown sugar mixture on high till mixture boils. Stir once to dissolve sugar and microwave again on medium-low heat for 4 minutes or until mixture is golden brown. Stir in vanilla and soda. Pour over pretzel mixture. Toss to coat evenly. Microwave on high uncovered 4 to 5 minutes, or till lightly glossed, stirring twice. Spoon onto wax paper to cool. Break into pieces. Store in tight container. (Can be frozen in ziplock bags.)

Jeanne and Ben Carr
Lexington, Kentucky
University of Kentucky Wildcat Fans

Spinach Dip

1 cup mayonnaise
1 cup sour cream
1 medium onion, chopped fine or
        1 envelope Lipton onion cup of soup
8-ounce can water chestnuts
1 package Knorr Vegetable Soup mix
1 package frozen spinach

Chop water chestnuts in blender. If using onions, chop fine. Drain spinach very dry and chop in blender (uncooked). Dip is green in color and is good with raw veggies or chips.

Kelli Oakley
Lexington, Kentucky
Henry Clay Blue Devil Fan
Murray State University Racer Fan

Beer Cheese

16-ounce shredded Cheddar cheese
16-ounce shredded Swiss cheese
1 clove garlic, crushed and minced
1 tablespoon dry mustard
2 teaspoons Worcestershire sauce
⅛ teaspoon cayenne red pepper
    (more or less to taste)
8-ounce beer

In a mixing bowl or food processor, combine all ingredients; mix well until smooth. Store in the refrigerator in a covered jar or crock. Makes about 3 cups. Serve with crackers.

Bryan Houck
Lexington, Kentucky
University of Kentucky Wildcat Fan

Pineapple Pecan Cheese Ball

Two 8-ounce packages cream cheese,
    softened
1 cup crushed pineapple, drained
¼ cup chopped green peppers
¼ cup chopped onions
1 tablespoon seasoned salt
1½ cups chopped pecans

Combine all ingredients except one cup of pecans. Mix well. Form into a ball. Roll the formed ball in the remaining pecans until completely covered. Refrigerate. Better if ball has set overnight.

Sonja Gaddie
Georgetown, Kentucky
Scott County High School Cardinal Fan

Cardinal Chicken Bites

1 pound boneless skinless chicken breast
1 tablespoon garlic powder
1 tablespoon onion powder
1 tablespoon pepper
2 teaspoons seasoned salt
1 teaspoon paprika
1 small onion, cut into strips
15 jalapeno peppers, halved and seeded
1 pound sliced bacon, halved width-wise
1 jar of favorite blue cheese dressing

Cut chicken into 2-inch by 1½-inch strips. In a large resealable plastic bag, combine the garlic powder, onion powder, pepper, seasoned salt and paprika; add chicken and shake to coat. Place a chicken and onion strip in each jalapeno half. Wrap each with a piece of bacon and secure with toothpicks. Grill, uncovered, over indirect medium heat for 18 to 20 minutes or until chicken juice runs clear and bacon is crisp, turning once. Serve with blue cheese dressing.

David Hurst
Louisville, Kentucky
University of Louisville Cardinal Fan

Greg Schmidt, son of Irv Schmidt, grills bologna at Fischer's Packing Company caboose. Schmidt is a 1989 graduate of the University of Louisville and has been tailgating since he was a boy.

Hot Artichoke Spread

14-ounce can artichoke hearts,
    drained and chopped
¾ to 1 cup mayonnaise
1 cup grated parmesan cheese
½ teaspoon garlic salt
Dash of lemon juice

Combine all ingredients and mix well. Spoon into a lightly greased 3-cup casserole. Bake at 350 degrees for 25 minutes. Serve with assorted crackers.

Makes about 2½ cups. This is a great dish.

**Peggy Graviss
Bowling Green, Kentucky
Western Kentucky University Hilltopper Fan**

Cheerleaders visit the Graviss tailgate party at Western Kentucky University. John Grider and Bob Kirby pose with the squad.

Homemade Pimento Cheese

1½ cups of mayonnaise
4-ounce jar diced pimento, drained
1 tablespoon finely grated onion
1 teaspoon Worcestershire sauce
8-ounce block extra sharp cheddar cheese, shredded
8-ounce block sharp cheddar cheese, shredded
½ cup pickled jalapeno pepper slices, drained and chopped

Combine first 4 ingredients in a large bowl; stir in cheeses. Stir in chopped pepper. Spoon cheese into gift jars. Store in refrigerator.

Carol Gabbard
Lexington, Kentucky
University of Kentucky Wildcat Fan

Taco Dip

1 pound hamburger, brown and drain
1 package of taco seasoning mix
1 can tomato soup
8-ounce carton sour cream
Cheddar cheese

Mix hamburger, taco seasoning mix, tomato soup and sour cream in a casserole dish. Top with shredded cheddar cheese. Bake at 350 degrees for about 20 minutes or until bubbly. Uncover for the last 5 minutes. Serve with tortilla chips.

Sherri Beth McKee
Georgetown, Kentucky
Scott County High School Cardinal Fan

Buffalo Chicken Dip

3 large boneless chicken breasts, boiled or baked
3 stalks celery, chopped
12-ounce bottle red hot sauce
Two 8-ounce packages of cream cheese
8-ounce ranch or blue cheese dressing

Boil or bake the chicken breasts. In a pan, pour in red hot sauce and celery and cook until tender. Slowly add the cream cheese, stirring often. Add 1 cup of dressing, stir. Finally, add cut up pieces of chicken. Stir well. Pour into a 2 quart or larger casserole. Bake at 400 degrees for 30 minutes. Serve with celery, tortillas, low carb bagels, or crackers.

Amy McGuire
Georgetown, Kentucky
Scott County High School Cardinal Fan

They call themselves "college football tailgate fans" -- they tailgate everywhere there is a game but cheer for only a few! From left to right are Matt Andrews, Svend Jansen, Nick Adams, Kyle Reh and Karrie Harper, all of Louisville.

Red-Hot Buffalo Chicken Dip

Two 13-ounce cans of chicken
1 cup ranch dressing
1 cup Frank's red hot (we use buffalo style)
Two 8-ounce blocks of cream cheese
2 cups of shredded cheddar cheese

Mix it all up and bake for about 40 minutes at 350 degrees. (You can also sprinkle cheese on top.) Serve with Fritos, Tostitos, celery, or whatever.

Karrie Harper
University of Kentucky Wildcat Fan
Indianapolis Colts Fan

Kyle Reh and Karrie Harper, Louisville, attended the University of Kentucky's 2006 Music City Bowl game in Nashville, TN against Clemson University. UK won 28-20.

Fiesta Crab Dip

8-ounce package cream cheese, softened
8-ounce cup picante sauce
8-ounce package imitation crabmeat, chopped
1 cup shredded cheddar cheese
½ cup thinly sliced green onions
2 tablespoons sliced ripe olives
2 tablespoons diced fresh tomato
2 tablespoons minced fresh cilantro
Tortilla chips, assorted crackers, or fresh veggies

In a mixing bowl, combine the cream cheese and picante sauce. Add crab, cheese, and onions. Mix well, cover, and refrigerate. Transfer to a serving bowl. Sprinkle with olives, tomato and cilantro. Serve with chips, crackers, or veggies. Makes 3 cups.

Sharon Hawkins
Georgetown, Kentucky
Scott County High School Cardinal Fan

KISS Sausage Balls

1 pound sausage, "Zesty" is best
1½ cups Bisquick
1 cup mozzarella cheese, small cubes are best but a thick shredded variety will do
⅛ teaspoon garlic powder

Combine ingredients. Mix thoroughly. Shape into balls – about jawbreaker size. Golf ball size is too big and gumball size is too small unless using them in a sauce. Place on a cookie sheet about ½ inch apart. Cook in preheated oven at 400 degrees until just done – approximately 10-15 minutes. Serve alone or with your favorite BBQ sauce. We like to add a little brown sugar, red pepper, ground clove, and liquid smoke to plain BBQ sauce for some zip. These are so simple you can make them ahead of time or before you walk out the door!

Cheryl Weaver and daughters, Kori, Koti and Kadi
Shelbyville, Kentucky

Jerry's Screamin' Jalapeños

24 large jalapeños
8 ounces cream cheese, softened
Sun-dried tomatoes
2 teaspoons fresh basil, minced
2 garlic cloves, minced
I pound bacon

Cut a slit along the side of the jalapeños and set aside. In a bowl, mix cream cheese, basil, sun dried tomatoes and garlic. Stuff jalapeños with the cheese mixture and wrap each one with a half piece of bacon. Either metal or wooden skewers can be used but metal works the best. This allows you to prep the jalapeños the night before. Grill the jalapeños until the bacon is cooked. One item not mentioned is the beer one may need to cool their palette.

Jerry Hibbard
Lexington, Kentucky
University of Kentucky Wildcat Fan

Cheesy Linebacker Dip

14¾-ounce can artichoke hearts, drained
    and finely chopped
2 cloves garlic, pressed
I cup shredded Mozzarella cheese
½ cup grated parmesan cheese
½ cup mayonnaise

Preheat oven to 350 degrees. Combine all ingredients and blend well. Spread into an ovenproof serving dish. Bake for 25-30 minutes or until golden and bubbly. Serve with assorted crackers.

Nancy Mueller
Georgetown, Kentucky
Scott County High School Cardinal Fan

Taco Dip

8-ounce sour cream
8-ounce whipped cream cheese
I package taco seasoning

Mix all ingredients with a hand mixer until well blended. Spread onto a large plate or 13x9x2 dish. Top with your favorite taco toppings such as shredded cheese, lettuce, tomatoes, olives and onions. Serve with bite size tortilla chips.

Holly Lynn
Lexington, Kentucky
University of Kentucky Wildcat Fan

Bean Dip

2 cans Frito bean dip
8-ounce container sour cream
I onion, chopped
Chopped lettuce
2 medium tomatoes, chopped
½ package taco seasoning
Jalapenos
Black olives
Shredded cheddar cheese
Tortilla chips

On a cookie sheet spread out bean dip, sprinkle taco seasoning, layer sour cream, layer tomatoes, layer lettuce, layer jalapenos, or black olives, and cover with cheese. Dig in with a chip!

Lori Pendleton
Georgetown, Kentucky
Scott County High School Cardinal Fan

Spicy Meatballs

2 small onions, finely chopped and divided
2 tablespoons olive oil
10 ¾-ounce can tomato puree
1 ¼ cup water
¼ cup red wine vinegar
2 to 3 tablespoons Worcestershire sauce
2 teaspoons brown sugar
½ teaspoon salt
½ teaspoon chili powder
¼ teaspoon garlic powder
1 pound ground beef
1 small jalapeno pepper, seeded and finely
    chopped
1 large egg, lightly beaten
½ cup cracker meal
½ cup ketchup
1 teaspoon salt
1 teaspoon pepper
½ teaspoon hot sauce

Saute chopped onion in olive oil over medium-high heat for five minutes. Add tomato puree and next 8 ingredients. Bring to a boil, reduce heat, and simmer for 1 hour, stirring every 15 minutes. Combine ground beef, onion, jalapeno pepper, egg, cracker meal, ketchup, salt, and pepper. Shape into ½-inch balls and place on a lightly greased rack in a roasting pan. Bake at 350 degrees for 20 minutes or until pink is gone. Add to sauce in skillet and stir gently. Stir in hot sauce just before serving.

Kelli Oakley
Lexington, Kentucky
Henry Clay Blue Devil Fan
Murray State University Racer Fan

Stuffed Mushrooms Cajun Style

**30 medium sized mushrooms,
    stalks reserved
2 ounces butter
I onion, finely diced
I green bell pepper, finely diced
I pound Andouille sausage meat
I pint beef stock
I ounce tomato paste or puree
4 ounces bread crumbs, dried
Salt and pepper to taste**

Finely chop the mushroom stalks, melt the butter in a suitable sized pan and sauté the onion until translucent. Add the bell pepper and the mushroom and continue the sauté with out color. Remove the vegetables from the pan and reserve, add the sausage to the hot pan and sauté till brown. Return the vegetables to the sauté pan, add the stock, and tomato puree mix thoroughly. Then, use the bread crumb to bind the mass together. Adjust the seasoning and spoon the mixture into the empty mushroom caps and set onto a lightly oiled proof tray or dish. Place in a preheated oven at 400 degrees and cook. When cooked remove from oven and garnish with chopped parsley and serve. Note: You may adjust the spicy heat of the stuffing with the use of cayenne pepper if required. Serves 30.

**Chef David Dodd
Floyd Knobs, Indiana
Chicago Bears Fan**

Cardinal Cheese Spread

1½ cups mayonnaise
4-ounce diced pimentos, drained
1 tablespoon finely grated onion
1 teaspoon Worcestershire sauce
8-ounce block extra-sharp cheddar cheese, shredded
8-ounce block sharp cheddar cheese, shredded
½ cup pickled jalapeno pepper slices, drained and chopped

Combine first 4 ingredients in a large bowl; stir in cheeses. Stir in chopped pepper. Spoon cheese into gift jars. Store in refrigerator.

Nora Bailey
Louisville, Kentucky
University of Louisville Cardinal Fan

Rick Harned parked cars at the University of Louisville/West Virginia game on November 2, 2006. Harned said he helps Boy Scout Troop #1, Louisville, raise money parking over 700 cars at $10 each, during each home game.

Nacho Dip

16-ounce salsa, Chi Chi's or homemade
16-ounce Cheese Whiz
1 pound hot sausage, crumbled

Cook sausage and drain. Add Cheese Whiz and salsa and serve warm with tortilla chips.

Ryan Oakley
Lexington, Kentucky
Murray State University Racer Fan

Curried Chicken Wings

14 chicken wings
½ cup yogurt
1½ teaspoon curry powder
Salt to taste
Hot sauce (dab)

Cook for 30 minutes at 475 degrees.

Liz Browning
Sandston, Virginia

Corn Hole Sausage Dip

**I pound sausage with sage, brown and
drain**
16 ounces cream cheese
I can Rotel tomatoes

Mix all three ingredients. Heat and serve.

Jackie Allen
Midway, Kentucky
University of Kentucky Wildcat Fan

*Corn Hole players posed for a quick photo during a University
of Kentucky football game. From left to right are Jimmy Ball
of Lexington, Paul Miller of Georgetown, and Gary McKee of
Lexington.*

Fruit Dip

1 small can cream of coconut
1 small Velveeta cheese
1 small Cool Whip

Blend cream of coconut and cheese (do not blend too long). Add Cool Whip. Serve with an assortment of fruit.

Peggy Reid
Sandston, Virginia
Virginia Tech University Hokie Fan

Mango Dip

8 ounces cream cheese
1 jar mango chutney
½ cup coconut
½ cup peanuts

Spread cream cheese on plate and spread chutney on top. Sprinkle coconut and peanuts on top.

Peggy Reid
Sandston, Virginia
Virginia Tech University Hokie Fan

Mexi Bites

8 ounces cream cheese, room temperature
1 can (3 ounces) green chilies, drained and
diced
2 tablespoons minced onion
1 pkg. 10 count flour tortillas
1 jar of favorite salsa

Combine cream cheese, chilies, onions in medium bowl. Spread mixture on tortilla and roll into shape. Place in shallow dish in one layer and cover with damp cloth. Refrigerate for at least one hour. When ready to serve, cut into slices, cross-wise, in 1-inch slices. Serve with salsa.

Rebecca Allison
Lexington, Kentucky
University of Kentucky Wildcat Fan

University of Kentucky students enjoy tailgating during a football game in 2006. From left to right were Brandon Henderson, Crystal Anderson, Ashley Page, Sarah Combstock, Alex Marks and Rebecca Allison.

Sausage Stars

1 pound ground sausage, browned &
 drained
1 cup ranch dressing
1½ cup shredded Colby Jack cheese
1½ cup shredded sharp Cheddar cheese
1 package wonton wrappers

Place wonton wrappers in mini muffin pans to form a cup and bake no more than 5 minutes in 350-degree oven. Watch carefully. Mix sausage, ranch dressing, Colby jack cheese and cheddar cheese. Fill wonton cups with sausage mixture and bake just long enough to melt cheese, 1 to 2 minutes. Garnish with black olives slices if desired.

Kim Novicki
Louisville, Kentucky
University of Kentucky Wildcat Fan

In 2005, Home City Ice started delivering 132,000 pounds of ice at the University of Kentucky at 5:15 a.m. for a 12:30 p.m. football game. This, according to supervisor Billy Campbell, included 15 workers driving three to four forklifts to deliver to 45 different locations in the stadium. From left to right are Matt Lewin, Edgewood, KY; Billy Campbell, Lexington; and Aaron Ferrell, Madisonville, KY.

Fresh Pineapple Salsa

½ of a fresh pineapple, diced small
5 medium Roma tomatoes, diced ¼ inch
  thick
3 tablespoons cilantro, chopped
1 tablespoon jalapeno, chopped
½ red onion, diced fine
1 teaspoon salt
2 tablespoons brown sugar
¼ black pepper, ground

Mix all ingredients together in a stainless steel or glass bowl. Cover and store in the refrigerator for 1 hour before serving.

Chef David Dodd
Floyd Knobs, Indiana
Chicago Bears Fan

Scotch Eggs

6 large eggs, hard-boiled and peeled
1 pound sausage (mild or hot, your choice)
½ cup flour
Your favorite dipping sauce

Dry eggs with paper towels. Roll in flour. Wrap eggs in sausage till covered. Deep fry to a dark golden brown. Drain on paper towels. Delicious and convenient cold, but can warm them at the edge of your grill while other stuff is cooking. I like to dip them in honey mustard sauce or just plain ketchup.

Mary Platt Clements
Versailles, Kentucky
University of Kentucky Wildcat Fan

38

Mango and Tangerine Salsa

8 ounces orange juice
5 mangoes, diced small
4 ounces tangerine oranges, segmented
    and diced
4 ounces mango chutney
½ cup cilantro, chopped
1 red bell pepper, diced small
1 teaspoon salt
1 teaspoon cayenne pepper
2 ounces brown sugar
1 tablespoon cornstarch, slurry

Bring the orange juice, brown sugar, cayenne pepper, and salt to a boil and thicken with the cornstarch slurry. Pour the hot mixture over the remaining ingredients and mix. Serves 20.

Chef David Dodd
Floyd Knobs, Indiana
Chicago Bears Fan

Spiced Pecans

¾ stick of butter
1 egg white
1 cup sugar
½ teaspoon salt
¼ teaspoon cinnamon
¼ teaspoon cloves
¼ teaspoon allspice
1 pound pecans

Heat oven to 300 degrees. Melt butter in a 9 x 13 pan and set aside. Beat egg white until stiff. In a separate bowl, mix sugar, salt, cinnamon, cloves, and allspice. Stir mixture into egg white (mixture will be stiff; you can divide it). Add pecans to sugar and spices and coat. Add coated pecans to melted butter and spread evenly. Bake 50 minutes. Stir twice during cooking. Remove to paper towel lined cookie sheet.

Linda Gray
Lexington, Kentucky
Henry Clay High School Blue Devil Fan
Murray State University Racer Fan
University of Kentucky Wildcat Fan

Ruffaging the Kicker

Salads – Hot & Cold

Grannie Charles' Chicken Salad

8 chicken breasts, boneless
½ cup pecans, optional
1 cup celery, diced
½ cup green olives
1 cup sweet pickles
2 cups Miracle Whip or mayonnaise,
       whichever you prefer
Green grapes, optional

Cook chicken and cut into small pieces. Add pecans, celery, olives and sweet pickles. Mix together with Miracle Whip or mayonnaise. Add grapes. Refrigerate and serve.

Louise "Grannie" Charles
Lexington, Kentucky

Louise Charles, left, takes a ride with Georgia Bulldog fan Debbie Shealy of Kennesaw, Georgia in her new Harley tailgate golf cart. Louise, of Lexington, is Debbie's grandmother and is a University of Kentucky Wildcat fan.

Bonsai Salad

¾ pound capellinne pasta, cooked
¼ red bell pepper, julienned
¼ yellow pepper, julienned
½ cup celery, bias cut
½ cup carrot, julienned
½ cup shiitake mushrooms, sliced and
    sautéed
½ cup pea pods, julienned
8 ounces chicken tenders, grilled and sliced
1 ounce sesame oil
1½ ounces soy sauce
¼ ounce ginger, ground
2 ounces oyster sauce
2 tablespoons parsley, chopped
3 ounces vegetable oil
1 ounce brown sugar
1 ounce rice wine vinegar

Mix and toss first 8 ingredients; set aside. In a small bowl, combine remaining ingredients and pour over salad.

Chef David Dodd
Floyd Knobs, Indiana
Chicago Bears Fan

Pre-Game 7-Up Salad

2 small boxes lemon Jello
2 cups boiled water
One 16-ounce 7-Up
1 large can crushed pineapple, drain but
    keep juice
1 cup pineapple juice
2 to 3 bananas
1 tablespoon sugar
1 tablespoon flour
1 egg yolk

Mix Jello, water, 7-Up, and juice; place in the bottom of a large bowl and refrigerate. Slice bananas and place on top of Jello mixture. Cook pineapple juice, sugar, flour, and egg yolk until thick. Pour over bananas and place back in refrigerator. Serve cold.

Allie Leffler
Louisville, Kentucky
University of Louisville Cardinal Fan

Walnut Chicken Salad

3 cups chicken, cooked and chopped
2 to 3 stalks fresh celery, chopped
1 tart apple, chopped
½ cup walnuts, chopped
¾ cup mayonnaise

Combine all ingredients and refrigerate. Note: May substitute almonds for walnuts and grapes for apples.

Steve Leffler
Elizabeth, Indiana
Indiana University Hoosier Fan

Cardinal Coleslaw

1 head of cabbage
1 tablespoon sugar
¼ cup tarragon vinegar
1 grated carrot (optional)
½ cup Marzetti slaw dressing
½ to ¾ cup mayonnaise
Salt and pepper

Shred cabbage as fine as possible. Add other ingredients and mix well. Better if refrigerated for several hours.

Joe Pat Covington
Lexington, Kentucky
Scott County High School Cardinal Fan

Some tailgate parties just keep growing with the years. Patti Howard, Lexington, said she has been tailgating ever since Commonwealth Stadium opened at the University of Kentucky, and new tailgaters join every year. Her group includes, from left to right, Wanda Howard, Tina Wright, Lora Browning, Patti Howard, Tami Smith, Barb Spitz and Joe McGlone.

Thai Cucumber Salad

3 pounds cucumber, peeled, seeded and
   sliced
½ red onion, fine julienned
½ yellow bell pepper, julienned
8 ounces cellophane noodles, cooked
3 ounces cilantro, chopped
Salt and pepper to taste

   Thai Dressing Ingredients:
½ cup coconut milk, canned
¼ cup peanut butter
I tablespoon soy sauce
I tablespoon lime juice
I teaspoon brown sugar
I teaspoon ginger, ground
½ tablespoon red pepper flakes
¼ teaspoon salt

Combine first 5 ingredients and add salt and pepper
to taste. In a small mixing bowl, blend remaining
ingredients and pour over salad. Serves 20.

Chef David Dodd
Floyd Knobs, Indiana
Chicago Bears Fan

Taffy Apple Salad

½ cup sugar
1 egg
2 tablespoons cider vinegar
8 ounces Cool Whip
8-ounce can crushed pineapple
4 cups diced red apples (unpeeled)
1 cup raw or Spanish peanuts

Combine flour, sugar, egg, vinegar and juice from pineapple. Cook over low heat until thick. Cool. Pour over apples, pineapple and peanuts. Fold in Cool Whip. Store in the fridge until ready to eat!

(Tip: I buy the bag of sliced red apples at Kroger's, and one bag is just enough for one recipe.)

Leslie Hughes
Georgetown, Kentucky
Scott County High School Cardinal Fan
University of Kentucky Wildcat Fan

Left to right, Dawn Eads, Sam Adkins and Ernie Crawford warm up during a University of Kentucky football game. Crawford said he had been tailgating for 40 years and misses everyone when the football season ends each year.

Marinated Pasta Salad

12-ounce package tri-colored vegetable
    rotini pasta, cook according to
    package directions
¾ cup green pepper, chopped
¾ cup sweet onion, preferably Vidalia,
    chopped
Salt substitute, preferably Mrs. Dash
Pepper
15-ounce can green beans, French or
    Italian
15-ounce can dark red kidney beans
15-ounce can garbanzo beans (chick peas)
15-ounce can black beans
15-ounce can wax beans
1 ½ half cups sugar
1 cup cider vinegar
⅓ cup balsamic vinegar
⅔ cup vegetable oil

Drain the cooked rotini. Quickly mix the chopped green pepper and onion with the hot rotini in a very large bowl. Drain the cans of beans, but do not add yet. To make marinade, gradually add the sugar to the vinegars, stirring until dissolved. Add the vegetable oil and mix well. Add the drained beans to the pasta; sprinkle Mrs. Dash (or salt substitute) and pepper over the beans. Stir the marinade one more time and pour over everything. Mix well. Cover with plastic wrap and put in the refrigerator to chill. You can make this several days in advance and stir it once a day. The longer it sits, the better it gets. This makes enough for a crowd.

By varying the vegetables, you get a different flavor. One friend uses corn, baby lima beans, and frozen peas instead of black beans, wax beans and garbanzo beans and adds pimentos. Another friend adds lots of black olives to the original recipe.

Wilda Woodyard
Simpsonville, Kentucky
Virginia Tech University Hokie Fan

Waldorf Chicken Salad

2 cups canned chunk white chicken,
    drained
2 cups diced apples
2 tablespoons lemon juice
1½ cups celery, chopped
1 cup pecans, chopped
1½ cups white raisins
1 cup mayonnaise

Toss apples with lemon juice. Combine with remaining ingredients and refrigerate before serving.

Steve Leffler
Elizabeth, Indiana
Indiana University Hoosier Fan

Broccoli Salad

4 cups raw broccoli florets, cut bite-size
⅓ cup purple onion, chopped
½ cup dark raisins
1 cup salted (shelled) sunflower seeds
9 strips bacon, cooked crisp and crumbled
1½ cups mayonnaise
2 tablespoons sugar
1 tablespoon white vinegar

Combine broccoli, onion, raisins, sunflower seeds and bacon. Mix mayonnaise, sugar and vinegar and stir into the broccoli mixture. Serves 6.

Wini Humphrey
Lexington, Kentucky
University of Kentucky Wildcat Fan

Hilltopper Tater Salad

8 medium potatoes
1½ cup mayonnaise
1 cup sour cream
1½ teaspoon horseradish
1 teaspoon celery seed
½ teaspoon salt
1 cup chopped fresh parsley
2 medium onions, finely minced

Peel potatoes and cut into ⅛-inch slices. Combine mayonnaise, sour cream, horseradish, celery seed, and salt; set aside. In another bowl, mix parsley and onions. In a large serving bowl, arrange a layer of potatoes; salt lightly. Cover with a layer of mayonnaise/sour cream mixture, then a layer of the onion mixture. Continue layers ending with parsley and onion. Do not stir. Cover and refrigerate at least 8 hours. Make the day before and it is especially delicious.

Shaun Coffey
Russell Springs, Kentucky
Western Kentucky University Hilltopper Fan
University of Kentucky Wildcat Fan

Big Red, the Western Kentucky University Hilltopper's mascot, signs autographs during the 2005 homecoming game. Big Red was celebrating his 25th birthday!

Sunflower Seed Salad

16-ounce package coleslaw mix
1 small bunch green onions, chopped
1 cup sunflower seeds
1 cup slivered almonds
2 packages beef flavored Ramen noodles
⅓ cup vinegar
½ cup sugar
¾ cup oil
Flavoring packets from Ramen noodles

Combine ingredients. Note: You may also use shredded carrots, chopped green pepper, or broccoli.

Granny Pat Marcum
Lexington, Kentucky
University of Kentucky Wildcat Fan
Henry Clay High School Blue Devil Fan
Murray State University Racer Fan

Dee's Tailgating Tater Salad

15-20 new (red) potatoes, cooked and
    diced
8-10 hard boiled eggs, chopped
1 large Vidalia onion, minced or chopped
5 stalks celery, chopped
6 tablespoons dill relish
1 large green pepper, chopped
Garlic salt, to taste
Pepper, to taste
Cayenne pepper
½ cup mayonnaise
¼ cup Miracle Whip
2 tablespoons yellow mustard

Blend first 8 ingredients together until all mixed. Blend together mayonnaise, Miracle Whip and mustard. Combine with potato mixture; chill and serve.

Dee McIntosh
Georgetown, Kentucky
Scott County High School Cardinal Fan

Multi-Layered Salad

1 head lettuce
1 16-ounce package frozen peas
1 medium onion, chopped
15-ounce can sliced black olives
8-ounce package of shredded cheese
2 cups mayonnaise or Miracle Whip
2 tablespoons sugar
8-10 slices of bacon fried crisp (you may
    use real bacon bits)
3 hard boiled eggs, chopped

Break lettuce in large bowl. Then layer peas, onions, and black olives over lettuce. Mix sugar and mayonnaise together and spread on top. Then sprinkle cheese over the dressing. Add crumbled bacon and chopped eggs. Refrigerate before serving.

Linda Bramham
Georgetown, Kentucky
Scott County High School Cardinal Fan

Hot Potato Salad

I tablespoon flour
10 new potatoes, cooked and cubed
I pound bacon, fried crisp
I cup mayonnaise
I cup onion
I pound Velveeta

Mix all of the above. Bake at 350 degrees for 30 minutes or until hot and bubbly.

In Memory of Sam Mays
Lexington, Kentucky
University of Kentucky Wildcat Fan

Tailgaters take a break before a University of Kentucky football game to play a new game called "ladders." Golf balls are attached at both ends of a two-inch string. These balls on a string are then thrown at a ladder, consisting of three rails. To score, you must wrap the ball and string around the different levels to accumulate points. Players include, from left to right, Vicki House, Louisville; Jack Buehner, Louisville; Rick Eckerle, Louisville; Kendle Payton, Louisville; James "Pappy" Lunceford, Louisville; Bobby Martin, Louisville; and Ron Shipley, Ekron.

"Bulldog" Potato Salad

10 pounds red new potatoes
8 hard boiled eggs
1 medium jar sweet diced pickles
½ cup diced celery
2 tablespoons onion flakes
½ cup mayonnaise
½ cup of mustard
Salt to taste

Peel, cube, and cook potatoes until tender. Drain and cool potatoes. Boil eggs and dice. Mix potatoes, eggs, celery, onion flakes, pickles, salt, mayonnaise, and mustard. Potato salad mixture should be a little soupy. Potato salad will soak up mayonnaise and mustard and will taste better if prepared the day before tailgating.

Eddie Oakley
Lexington, Kentucky
Henry Clay High School Blue Devil Fan
Murray State University Racer Fan

Turkey Salad

1 turkey breast
3 cups water
1 jar diced pimentos, drained
1 stalk celery, chopped
1 medium onion, chopped
Pickle relish
Salad dressing, or Miracle Whip

Bake turkey breast in water, covered at 325 degrees for about 4 hours (you want the breast real dry). Crumble and let cool. Add remaining ingredients.

Steve Leffler
Elizabeth, Indiana
Indiana University Hoosier Fan

Old Time Fruit Salad

3 eggs, beaten
¾ cup sugar
3 tablespoons soft butter
½ cup lemon juice
3 Gold Delicious apples, cored, peeled, chopped
3 Red Delicious apples, cored, peeled, chopped
1 bunch seedless green grapes, halved
1 bunch seedless red grapes, halved
20-ounce pineapple tidbits, drain
¾ cup chopped pecans
1½ cups mini marshmallows

Combine the eggs, sugar, and soft butter in a small saucepan. Stir in lemon juice. Cook over medium heat until thickened, stirring constantly. Refrigerate until cool. While sauce is cooling, chop apples (if they sit too long they will brown, so do AFTER making sauce). In a large serving bowl place all the fruit and marshmallows, then lightly mix. Pour the dressing over the fruit and fold in. Makes 12 servings. Once dressing is on salad, fruit will not brown for 2-3 days, due to lemon juice.

Liz Watson
Lexington, Kentucky
University of Kentucky Wildcat Fan

Thomas and King parks a bus at Commonwealth Stadium during most of the University of Kentucky football games entertaining employees, clients, friends and family. From left to right, attending the UK/University of Georgia game in 2006 is Hank Jones, Beth Waldrop, Jonathan Weatherby and Billy Hilliard, all of Lexington.

Pea Salad

2 cans peas with pearl onions, drained
1 small jar pimentos, drained
½ cup sliced celery
¼ cup chopped black olives
1 boiled egg, chopped
1 cup cheddar cheese, cubed
1 cup mayonnaise
Dash of lemon juice
Salt and pepper to taste

Combine peas, pimentos, celery, olives, egg, and cheddar cheese in a small bowl and mix together. In a small bowl, mix mayonnaise, lemon juice, salt, and pepper. Add to pea mixture and chill.

"I have been making this dish for over 20 years. It is my favorite pea salad recipe."

Linda Watkins
Lexington, Kentucky
University of Kentucky Wildcat Fan

Chicken Salad

3 chicken breasts, cooked and diced
⅓ cup celery, chopped
4-5 green onions
⅓ cup craisins
⅓ cup dried apricots
½ cup broken cashews
Mayonnaise
Salt
Pepper

Mix all with mayo, salt, and pepper to taste. Tasty on sandwich or bed of lettuce.

Peggy Reid
Sandston, Virginia
Virginia Tech University Hokie Fan

Granny Odella's Fruit Salad

**Juice from 15 oz. can of pineapple pieces
   or chunks
1 egg (beaten)
¾ cup sugar
1 tbs. flour
Assorted fruit**

Mix all ingredients and cook slowly until thick. Let cool. Pour over assorted chopped fruit of your choice (e.g., apples, oranges, pineapple, grapes and bananas).

**Leslie Hughes
Georgetown, Kentucky
Scott County High School Cardinal Fan
University of Kentucky Wildcat Fan**

Sally Simonton (a 1978 UK grad) helped park cars during a University of Kentucky football game in 2006. Simonton, who played on UK's softball team, said she parked cars during games and it assures her of a good spot at the game—on the field!

Hot Chicken Salad

2 cups chicken, cooked and chopped
2 cups celery, chopped
½ cup salted almonds, chopped
½ cup green pepper, chopped
2 tablespoons pimento, chopped
2 tablespoons minced onion
½ teaspoon salt
2 tablespoons lemon juice
½ cup mayonnaise
1 cup crushed potato chips

Blend chicken, celery, almonds, green pepper, pimento, onion, salt, lemon juice, and mayonnaise. Turn into buttered 1½-quart casserole. Top with grated cheese and crushed potato chips. Bake at 350 degrees for 25 minutes or until cheese is melted. Makes 6 to 8 servings.

Patty Cornett
Georgetown, Kentucky
Scott County High School Cardinal Fan

Frozen Salad

3 bananas
8-ounce package cream cheese, softened
1 large can crushed pineapple, drained
1 large can fruit cocktail, drained
1 large bottle maraschino cherries and
        juice
1 large Cool Whip

Mix bananas and cream cheese. Add all other ingredients. Put into a 9x13 pan and freeze. Remove from freezer 30 minutes before using.

Peggy Reid
Sandston, Virginia
Virginia Tech University Hokie Fan

Waldorf Salad

1 cup celery, diced
1 cup tart apples, diced
1 cup red grapes, halved
1 cup dried fruits, use craisins and
      dried apricots
½ cup walnuts
2 tablespoons orange zest
¾ cup mayonnaise
¼ cup cranberry juice

Mix all ingredients together and chill.

Peggy Reid
Sandston, Virginia
Virginia Tech University Hokie Fan

Marinated Vegetable Salad

1 pound broccoli
1 head cauliflower
2 or 3 large carrots, sliced
2 or 3 medium zucchini, sliced
2 small onions, cut into rings
⅔ cup mayonnaise
⅓ cup oil
⅓ cup apple cider vinegar
¼ cup sugar
2 teaspoons salt

Cut up vegetables. Mix last 5 ingredients and pour over vegetables. Chill and serve. Serves 12 to 16 people.

Pat Tuttle
Lexington, Kentucky

Orzo Salad

2 ½ pounds orzo, cooked
4 ounces sun-dried tomatoes, finely diced
1¾ cups feta cheese, crumbled
6 ounces Kalamati olives, sliced
1¼ cups spinach leaves, chopped
1 ounce olive oil, lemon flavored
½ cup white wine vinegar
1 red onion, thinly sliced
2 teaspoons sugar
Salt and pepper to taste

Add all the ingredients, except for the Orzo together in a large bowl and mix well. Season with the salt and pepper. Add the orzo and gently fold over to mix in the orzo. Allow to chill overnight to incorporate flavors. Serves 20.

Chef David Dodd
Floyd Knobs, Indiana
Chicago Bears Fan

Missy and Jett Mathews pose with some of the WKU cheerleaders.

Oriental Salad

16-ounce package cole slaw
2 packages Ramen noodles, without
    flavoring
1 tablespoon oil
2 tablespoons apple cider vinegar
3 tablespoons white sugar

Mix all ingredients together. Add more oil or vinegar to taste, if needed. Serve chilled.

Nancy Mueller
Georgetown, Kentucky
Scott County High School Cardinal Fan

Shredded Carrot Salad

1 pound grated carrots
1 large can pineapple tidbits
2 cans mandarin oranges
1 cup golden raisins
½ pound shredded coconut
8 ounces sour cream

Drain pineapple and oranges. Mix all ingredients. Add sour cream last and chill before serving.

Peggy Reid
Sandston, Virginia
Virginia Tech University Hokie Fan

Bowl Games

Soups, Chilis & Stews

Jim's Football Jambalaya

1½ to 2 pounds chicken, cooked, boned,
   and chopped
1½ pounds hot smoked sausage
1 pound smoked ham, diced
1 pound medium to large shrimp, shelled
1 pound salad shrimp
1 large onion, chopped
1 bell pepper, chopped
4 cloves garlic, minced
3 celery ribs, finely chopped
1 large can and 1 small can of tomato
   paste
1 small can tomato sauce
28-ounce can chopped tomatoes
4 cups chicken stock
2 tablespoons "Tiger Sauce"
1 tablespoon "Picka Peppa Sauce"
1 teaspoon Tabasco sauce
1 teaspoon cayenne pepper
1 teaspoon black pepper
1 teaspoon white pepper
1 teaspoon oregano
1 teaspoon thyme
2 whole bay leaves
Salt to taste
4 cups long grain rice, uncooked

Season the chicken meat with a little salt and pepper; set aside. Brown the sliced smoked sausage; pour off the fat and set aside. Sauté the onions, garlic, bell pepper, and celery until the onions turn translucent. Mix the tomato paste with the tomato sauce and brown until it just starts to caramelize. Add the caramelized tomato paste and chopped tomatoes to the sautéed vegetables, stirring well. Deglaze the tomato paste pan with a little of the chicken stock to the mixture; it should be fairly thick. Add the seasonings and salt to taste. Let this mixture cook for about 30 minutes at medium heat (stir to keep from burning). Add the meat (chicken, ham, and sausage) and cook for another 45 to 60 minutes at low to medium temperature. Add the shrimp 10 minutes before removing from the heat. Make sure the shrimp is cooked. Prepare the 4 cups of rice according to its directions. This should make 8 cups after cooking. Mix the rice with the rest of the ingredients, stirring well. Put the whole mess into a large baking dish and bake uncovered at 350 degrees for approximately an hour. It is best to bake on upper shelf of the over to keep bottom from burning. This can be frozen for a brief period.

Helen Hague
Lexington, Kentucky
University of Kentucky Wildcat Fan
Henry Clay High School Blue Devil Fan

Cardinal Surprise

1 pound bulk pork sausage
1 pound ground beef
1 envelope taco seasoning
4 cups of water
Two 16-ounce cans kidney beans,
    rinsed and drained
Two 15-ounce cans pinto beans, rinsed
    and drained
Two 15-ounce cans garbanzo beans,
rinsed and drained
Two 14½-ounce cans stewed tomatoes
Two 14½-ounce cans Mexican diced
    tomatoes, undrained
Sour cream
Shredded cheddar cheese
Sliced ripe olives (optional)

Cook sausage and beef over medium heat until no longer pink; drain. Add taco seasoning and mix well. Stir in the water, beans, tomatoes, and salsa. Bring to a boil. Reduce heat; simmer uncovered for 30 minutes or until heated through; stir occasionally. Garnish with sour cream, cheese, and black olives if desired. Keep warm on tailgating grill.

Melinda Hurst
Louisville, Kentucky
University of Louisville Cardinal Fan

Holly's Chili

1 pound ground beef
1 pound ground sausage (mild)
14.5 ounce can pinto beans
14.5 ounce can kidney beans (dark red or
    light)
29 ounce can tomato sauce
Salt and pepper to taste
Favorite chili seasoning to taste
Tortilla chips
Shredded cheddar cheese
Sour cream

Brown ground beef and sausage in skillet and drain. In large pot, add ground beef, sausage, beans, salt, pepper, and chili seasoning. Mix together and simmer for about 30 minutes. If using crockpot, cook on low for 4 hours. Serve in a bowl on a bed of tortilla chips. Top with cheese and sour cream.

Holly Lynn
Lexington, Kentucky
University of Kentucky Wildcat Fan

Kyle Hite, Findlay, OH, was recipient of one of the UK RV Roadcat Club grants. The grant is given to a student who is not a scholarship athlete. Hite, a kinesiology major, received a check for $2,500 from RV Club President Pete Owen, right.

Black Bean Soup

2 cans black beans (drained and washed)
1 can Mexican chopped tomatoes
1 can chopped tomatoes
1 small can chopped green chilies
1 can of corn (white or yellow, drained)
1 tablespoon cumin
1 tablespoon chili powder (season to taste)
1 teaspoon garlic
½ cup of chopped onion
½ cup chopped green peppers (optional)
1 can chili hot beans (optional)

Put all the ingredients in a crock pot and cook on high for 2 to 3 hours. It is like a chili with no meat, wonderful in the cooler days of tailgating, and very good!

Marilyn and Pete Owens
Lexington, Kentucky
Kentucky RoadCats President
University of Kentucky Wildcat Fans

Becke McGaughey, Somerset, bottom right, was recognized by the RV Roadcat Club for her five-year membership and hard work. She received a $120 gift certificate and a Wildcat print.

Seth's Tailgate Chili

1 pound ground beef or turkey
1 diced medium yellow onion, diced
½ teaspoon cumin
1 tablespoon minced garlic
1 tablespoon salt
½ teaspoon black pepper

Brown ground meat with above ingredients and drain. Then add:

1-14.5 ounce can diced tomatoes, then fill
    three times with water and add
1-15.5 ounce can kidney beans, drained
1-10 ¾ ounce can tomato puree
1-9 ounce domestic beer (sample
    remaining 3 ounces to check
    quality!)
1 medium onion, diced
1 teaspoon salt
1 teaspoon cumin
½ teaspoon garlic, minced
⅛ teaspoon cayenne pepper
1 packet Lawry's Chili Seasoning
2 tablespoons jalapeño peppers, finely
    chopped

Boil together for 20 minutes (30 minutes if using beer). Continue to simmer over low to medium heat 30 to 45 minutes, based on desired consistency. I recommend topping with white cheddar cheese and oyster crackers, although any cheese and crackers work!

NOTE: The beer and jalapeño peppers kick it up a notch, but you don't have to use them.

Seth Stallard
Lexington, Kentucky
University of Kentucky Wildcat Fan

Robert Escobedo, Lexington, stirred chili during a University of Kentucky football game. Escobedo, a chef by profession, has been tailgating for five years.

Hearty Potato Soup

15 ounces potatoes, chopped and boiled
    (or use leftover mashed potatoes)
½ cup chopped onion
½ cup chopped carrot
½ cup chopped celery
2 cups skim milk, warmed
1 cup frozen peas, thawed
½ teaspoon salt
¼ teaspoon celery seed
⅛ teaspoon dill seed
⅛ teaspoon white pepper
2-3 dashes hot sauce (like Tabasco)
¼ teaspoon Liquid Smoke

Garnish:
1 green onion, chopped
¼ cup red bell pepper, chopped

Spray a nonstick pot with a little nonstick spray and sauté the onion, carrot, and celery until the onion is slightly soft (about 3 to 5 minutes). Drain the potatoes and add to the vegetables. Stir in the warm milk (warm the milk in the microwave for 5 minutes). Add the peas and seasonings. Simmer for 20-30 minutes. Adjust seasoning to taste, ladle into bowls, garnish with chopped green onions and red bell pepper, and serve.

For potato-cheese soup, put 1½ ounces of fat-free cheddar cheese in the bottom of the bowls before serving.

Jayna Oakley
Lexington, Kentucky
University of Kentucky Wildcat Fan
Henry Clay High School Blue Devil Fan
Lafayette High School Lady General Fan

Jambalya

2 bunches of green onions
1 large onion
1 green pepper
1 teaspoon thyme
1 teaspoon parsley
Dash cayenne
2 bay leaves
Salt, pepper, garlic to taste
⅓ cup oil
5 large boneless chicken breasts
1 package of smoked sausage
1 pound ham, or may exchange ham for
    crab and shrimp
1 large can crushed tomatoes
1 can tomato paste
1 cup rice
1 cup water or wine

Chop all vegetables and meat. Cook rice according to package and set aside. Put oil in skillet and heat and sauté vegetables until translucent. Add chicken and cook until white and then add other meats and heat through. Put tomatoes and paste in a crock pot with spices. Add water or wine and heat. Add meat/veggies to crockpot. Slowly stir in rice. When the crockpot is hot throughout, turn down on low. This dish will be better the longer you allow it to cook. Serve Louisiana hot sauce on the side and French bread. If you don't have a plug-in at the tailgate spot, transfer to a pot that will fit inside another larger pot as a double boiler over your fire, grill, etc.

Peggy Gravis
Bowling Green, Kentucky
Western Kentucky University Hilltopper Fan

Peggy and Charlie Graviss—WKU Tailgate Queen and King!

Graviss family sets TALEgating tradition

Peggy and Charlie Graviss have been tailgating at Western Kentucky University for many years. Their daughter Missy cheered at WKU for five years and then coached for two. Their oldest son, Chuck, cheered one year when he returned from "Desert Storm." Their other son, Chris, was still in the Rangers at that time, but returned and graduated from WKU. Their three children and three in-laws, whom they met at school, are all WKU graduates. Their son-in-law, John, played basketball for the Hilltoppers.

Peggy and Charlie have always hosted the Cheer squad for the football tailgaters, along with anyone who wanted to eat...which usually turned into a bunch of hungry people! As a result, Peggy and Charlie fix about 30 gallons of seafood gumbo (a secret family recipe) for each homecoming! According to Peggy and Charlie, there are some people who only come to that game for the seafood gumbo! The Graviss' have won awards for many years for their tailgate dishes.

(Top left) Members of the Graviss family include, from left, Hank, Heather, Lucy and Chuck Graviss. (Bottom left) Chris Graviss and his son, Matthew, at a tailgate picnic at WKU. (Above) A future WKU Hilltopper, Jett, poses with dad John and mom Missy Mathews.

Spicy Sausage and Bean Soup

1 teaspoon olive oil
1 pound bulk hot sausage (see note)
1 small onion, chopped
2 garlic cloves, minced
Four 15½ ounces cans each Great
        Northern beans, undrained
Two 14½-ounce cans chicken broth
One 14½-ounce can diced tomatoes,
        undrained
1 teaspoon dried basil
½ teaspoon black pepper

In a large soup pot, heat the oil and cover over medium to high heat. Add the sausage, onion, and garlic. Cook for 5 to 6 minutes or until no pink remains in the sausage, stirring frequently to break up the meat. Add the remaining ingredients and bring to a boil. Reduce the heat to medium-low and simmer uncovered for 30 minutes.

NOTE: I like this soup spicy, but if you need to turn the heat down, use a mild sausage or even turkey sausage.

Walter Marcum
Lexington, Kentucky
Henry Clay High School Blue Devil Fan
University of Kentucky Wildcat Fan

Tailgate Chili

10 pounds ground beef, browned
2-3 quarts tomato juice (use more if you
    want it more soupy)
4 medium onions, chopped
6 packages Chili-O seasoning mix
1 gallon can Bush's chili beans
1 gallon can diced tomatoes
Mexene chili powder to taste
Salt and pepper to taste

Mix above ingredients in an 18-quart roaster; bring to a boil and reduce heat to a simmer for 2-3 hours for desired thickness. Stir often. Sometimes we cook this in a black iron pot over a wood fire or a propane cooker. Makes 18 quarts. This is a great crowd pleaser.

Dawn and George Eads
Lexington, Kentucky
University of Kentucky Wildcat Fans
Roadcats RV Club Members

George Eads checks some of his turkey legs during a University of Kentucky football game. Eads, who runs Cummins Grocery in Lexington, is known for his chili dogs.

South of the Louisville Border Chowder

½ cup onion, chopped
4 bacon strips, diced
2 tablespoons all-purpose flour
½ teaspoon ground cumin
½ teaspoon chili powder
⅛ teaspoon garlic powder
1 package frozen Southern-style hash
    brown potatoes
Two 14¾-ounce cans cream style corn
11-ounce can Mexicorn, drained
4 ounce chopped green chilies
¼ cup pearl onion
Sour cream and minced fresh cilantro,
    optional

In a Dutch oven or soup kettle, sauté onion and bacon until onion is tender and bacon is crisp. Stir in the flour, cumin, chili powder and garlic powder. Bring to a boil; cook and stir for 1 minute or until thickened. Stir in the hash browns, broth, cream corn, Mexicorn, chilies, and pearl onions. Bring to a boil. Reduce heat; simmer, uncovered, for 10 minutes or until heated through. Garnish with sour cream and cilantro, if desired. Makes 10 servings.

Jayna Oakley
Lexington, Kentucky
University of Kentucky Wildcat Fan
Henry Clay High School Blue Devil Fan
Lafayette High School Lady General Fan

Scott County "On Fire" 20 Hour Chili

2 tablespoons vegetable oil
2 pounds stew meat
I small onion, finely chopped
I garlic bulb, peeled and separated
Two cans of Bush's Chili Beans
Two 28-ounce cans of tomato sauce
2 small cans of tomato paste
⅓ jar jalapenos with juice, to taste

In a large skillet, heat up with oil. Place chopped onion and all garlic bulbs in skillet and cook until onions are translucent. Add stew meat and brown (do not completely cook). While beef is browning, pour I can each tomato sauce, tomato paste, and chili beans into a crock pot. Add meat mixture and mix thoroughly. Cover and let simmer on low for 8 hours. At this point, stir very gently a few times, cover again, and let simmer for another 8-9 hours. Stir gently again, adding the additional cans of tomato sauce and chili beans, and the jalapenos (if desired). Cover and simmer another 3 hours. At this point, remove lid and stir vigorously to completely mix all ingredients. If the mixture needs to be thicker, add the last can of tomato paste and let thicken for 5-10 minutes. Serve with shredded cheese, sour cream, and warm cornbread.

Nancy Mueller
Georgetown, Kentucky
Scott County High School Cardinal Fan

No Fuss Potato Soup

32-ounce package frozen hash brown
    potatoes
1 medium onion, chopped
14½-ounce can chicken broth
2 cups water
1 can cream of celery soup, undiluted
12-ounce can low-fat evaporated milk

Combine first four ingredients. Bring to a boil. Cover and reduce heat. Simmer for 30 minutes. Stir in soup and milk. Heat through.

Linda Oakley
Lexington, Kentucky
Henry Clay High School Blue Devil Fan
University of Kentucky Wildcat Fan
Lafayette High School Lady General Fan

A few tailgaters from UPS joined all their friends during a University of Kentucky football game last year. UPS delivered the game ball while friends and family cheered those UPS employees carrying it onto the field for the coin toss. Kneeling, left to right, is Lisa Oldham, Shaun Cooper, Joy Sanders, Judelle Conley, Matt Stevens, and standing, left to right, Jeremy Calhoun, Dale Stevens, Greg Patterson Markeeta Marcum, Jeff Oldham, Seth Oldham, Libby Marcum, Rondell Lawson, Jackie Lawson, Jeremy Jones, David Jones, Cindy Russell, Nettie Jones and Chuck Frazier.

Home and Heart Bean Soup

2 cups dry beans (may be assorted)
1 large can of tomatoes, chopped
1 large onion, diced
1 clove garlic, minced
1 ½ teaspoon salt
¼ teaspoon pepper
1 teaspoon chili powder
2 cups smoked ham, diced
2 cups smoked sausage, diced
2 to 3 cups cooked chicken, diced
3 tablespoons salad oil or bacon fat

Wash and pick over beans thoroughly. Soak beans overnight. Drain beans, rinse well, cover with 3 quarts of water. Simmer for 1 to 2 hours until beans are tender. Add tomatoes, onion, garlic, salt, pepper, and chili powder; cook for an additional 45 to 60 minutes. Add smoked ham, smoked sausage, chicken, and oil; cook for an additional 45 to 60 minutes.

Rebecca L. Tucker
Lexington, Kentucky

Chili Soup with Cheese

1 large onion, chopped
2 tablespoons butter or margarine
2½ teaspoons chili powder
½ teaspoon garlic salt
¼ teaspoon cumin
½ teaspoon Mexican oregano
12-ounce can whole tomatoes
15½ ounce can kidney beans
2 cups beef broth
2 cups cooked pork or beef, diced
Shredded cheddar cheese

In a large kettle, sauté onion in butter until tender. Stir in chili powder, garlic salt, cumin and oregano. Cook 1 minute. Add tomatoes, kidney beans, and beef broth. Bring to a boil, cover, and simmer 20 minutes. You may add vegetables or anything else you find left over in the refrigerator. Cover and simmer 30 minutes longer. At serving time, sprinkle shredded cheese generously over soup. Makes 6 to 8 servings.

Sandra Oppegard
Lexington, Kentucky

White Chili

1 tablespoon vegetable oil
1 medium onion, chopped
2 cans Northern beans
½ teaspoon garlic powder
1 pound chicken, cooked and shredded
One to two 15-ounce cans chicken broth
1 can green chilis, chopped
1 teaspoon salt
1 teaspoon ground cumin
1 teaspoon oregano
½ teaspoon black pepper
¼ teaspoon cayenne pepper
1 cup sour cream
½ cup whipping cream (optional)

Sauté onions in oil. Drain beans and chicken. Put all ingredients except sour cream and whipping cream in a soup pan. Simmer for 30 minutes. Remove from heat and add sour cream and whipping cream. Stir.

Carmen Wallin
Georgetown, Kentucky
Scott County High School Cardinal Fan

Onion Soup

2 Vidalia onions, thinly sliced
I teaspoon dried thyme
¼ cup beer
¼ cup brandy
2 ounces honey
I bay leaf
I quart brown chicken stock

Caramelize the onions in a little olive oil and butter (this is the secret to the soup). The onions should develop really good brown color. Add rest of ingredients, and simmer for 20 minutes. Adjust seasoning if needed. Top with old stale crusty bread, grated gruyere, and gouda cheese. Bake in oven until cheese is melted.

Peggy Reid
Sandston, Virginia
Virginia Tech University Hokie Fan

Black Bean Soup

8 ounces dried black beans
2 quarts chicken stock
I cup onions, chopped
½ cup carrots
⅓ cup celery, chopped
2 tablespoons butter
I clove garlic, minced
I cup ham, diced
I bay leaf
I sprig thyme or ¼ teaspoon dried thyme
Salt
Freshly ground pepper
I small green pepper, may use red or
    yellow

Ida Byrd
Lexington, Kentucky
University of Kentucky Wildcat Fan
Tates Creek High School Commodore Fan

Southwest Soup

1– 2 pounds ground beef
1 onion, chopped
1 can white shoe peg corn
1 large can diced tomatoes with peppers,
    or may use 2 cans Rotel tomatoes
1 can black beans
1 can chili beans
1 can water
1 package ranch dressing
1 package taco seasoning mix

Brown beef and onion; drain. In a large pan, add the browned beef, onion, and all other ingredients. Cook on medium heat about 15 minutes. Stir frequently. Lower heat to simmer and cook about 2 hours; stir occasionally. Serve with cheese and cornbread.

Sylvia Jackson
Lexington, Kentucky

Paul Miller, Georgetown, is a 15-years plus tailgater at the University of Kentucky. Miller built the UK cart he's sitting on.

Cabbage Soup

1 large onion, chopped
½ cup oil
6 medium tomatoes, peeled, seeded, and
    quartered
7½ cups chicken broth
1 small head cabbage
4 ounces vermicelli, broken in pieces
3 ounces cream cheese
Salt and pepper, to taste

Sauté onion in oil until lightly browned. Whirl tomatoes 2 to 3 seconds in a food processor. Add to onions with broth and bring to a boil. Simmer 1½ hours. Remove outer leaves of cabbage; shred and add to soup with vermicelli. Cook, (stirring every 15 minutes) or until vermicelli is tender. Blend cheese with a little milk. Work into soup until well blended. Season with salt and pepper.

Peggy Reid
Sandston, Virginia
Virginia Tech University Hokie Fan

Chili – It's a Way of Life

My chili is based on a traditional CASI mix. CASI is the Chili Appreciation Society International, the major challenger to the International Chili Society in competitive chili cook-offs. Both organizations insist on a "meat and gravy" chili, with no beans, pasta, or other fillers. My traditional chili is augmented with red beans to make a non-competition, or "eatin'-style" chili. Ingredients are simple. It's mostly about technique. I like to cook the beans separately and add them to the chili mix at the end. Adding them too early, especially if tomatoes have been used, will toughen the beans. So, first things first:

First, Let's Make The Beans (one crock-pot sized recipe)

Day 1

Soak one pound of small red beans in one scant teaspoon of baking soda overnight; this will reduce the gassiness. These are the small beans used in Cajun beans and rice, not the large red kidney beans. Pintos can be substituted; Anasazi beans are an excellent alternative.

Day 2

Drain and rinse the beans (yeah, you lose some protein, but you also lose some of the complex sugars that cause gas.) Cover the beans with fresh water plus a can of reduced sodium chicken stock and place over a medium high heat until the water reaches a low boil. Turn down to a simmer immediately. While the beans are heating, finely chop one-half a medium onion (you will use the rest later) and sauté it in a tiny bit of olive oil until the onion becomes translucent. Three minutes before

Tom Jones, Lexington, Kentucky, gets ready to man the grill during a University of Kentucky football game.

Chili – It's a Way of Life (continued)

the onion is ready, stir in one or two tablespoons of chopped garlic. You don't want to cook the garlic too much; it will lose its flavor. Add the cooked onion and garlic to the bean pot.

Now it's time to spice the beans. Add about a tablespoon of fresh chili powder. Use a medium-red powder, not a chocolate brown one. Add one teaspoon of white pepper if you have it; black pepper will do. Add one scant teaspoon of mustard powder (or one heaping teaspoon of prepared mustard.) Cover and let simmer for at least an hour and a half. Stir and taste to check the spicing. It will probably seem pretty mild, but remember that it will be added to a heavily spiced meat and gravy. It's important to avoid acids (like tomatoes) since they toughen the beans. Avoid adding salt. It can always be added at the last minute, but it can never be removed.

Now for the chili itself. This can be prepared in parallel with the beans. The first and most important step is the selection of the meat. Tip roast, top round, or even chuck roast will work fine. Avoid ground beef unless you have a butcher that knows what a "chili grind" is. Pre-packaged ground beef is too finely ground to make real chili. Very lean cuts should be avoided; some marbling is needed to make proper gravy. For competition, the meat needs to be hand-cut into 3/8-inch cubes. You don't have to be perfect. For one large crock-pot, use two pounds of meat.

Place the cubed meat in a big bowl and add the gravy spicing, Two tablespoons ground comino (cumin), two tablespoons red chili powder, and a thickener. My favorite thickener is rice flour. You need only about one tablespoon of rice flour for two pounds of meat. You need a bit more with other thickeners. Unbleached wheat flour or masa is fine. The masa adds a corn flavor that some people love, but it doesn't thicken as well as rice flour. Finely ground corn flour is good if you can find it. Never use anything that says "self-rising"! Some people like more cumin and less chili powder. This is a matter of taste.

Stir the meat and spices together until you have a reasonably even coating on the meat. Heat a large skillet with one tablespoon of olive oil over medium heat. Add all the meat that will fit in a single layer. Sauté until browned or grayed (the color will depend on the spice mix.) The main function of this step is to produce a roux, from which the chili will derive its flavor and texture.

Don't try to cook the meat all the way through. Don't let the spices burn, you may have to adjust the heat. When the meat is browned, move it to another pot (don't add it to the beans yet!) Add a bit more oil between batches if needed. Brown all the meat. When you move the meat, scrap up as much of the coating off the pan as you can; we do not want to burn the roux! Add the scrapings to the pile of meat.

Move the chili pot to the burner and add some liquid to just cover the meat. Chicken stock is good. For competition I use one can of beer (bock style), plus chicken stock. If you use canned stocks, be sure you use the low-sodium varieties. Salt toughens meat as surely as acid toughens beans. Bring the chili pot to a simmer and cover.

Prepare an onion and garlic mix exactly the same way you did for the beans and add to the chili.

Now for the first spice load. A teaspoon of light red

chili powder, a teaspoon of good paprika and one of cayenne is a good start. Remember that spices added early will weaken with cooking. For the very best chili, now is the time to prepare a couple of fresh roasted ancho, poblano, or even green peppers (one green pepper is plenty). The purpose of roasting is to remove the pepper's skin. The easiest way is to blister it off with a propane torch. If you have a gas range, you can skewer the pepper and roast it over an open flame. It only takes a few seconds for the skin to start blistering. Scrub the blackened skin off with a vegetable brush. Split the pepper, remove the seeds if desired (they contain a lot of heat), and dice the flesh. Add the peppers to the chili. Also add

The Ellis Family poses during an Eastern Kentucky University football game. Their oldest son, Adam, was quarterback for the Colonels. Left to right are Teresa, Keith, Amy, Bryon and Blake (in helmet).

your secret ingredient, two dried or canned chipotlé peppers. These will probably dissolve in the chili if you stir fairly often, but you may want to leave them whole and remove them later if you don't want too much of their special, smoky fire.

Simmer the chili for an hour (keep it barely bubbling and stir frequently). Check the spicing. If you want to add heat, you can use a bit of Louisiana hot sauce, cayenne pepper, or the liquid from canned chipotlé peppers. It's too late to add raw chili powder. Chili powder takes a while to cook, and it is bitter if undercooked. Remember you will be adding the beans; check their spicing too. I like to add spicy chili to mild beans, some of this character will remain even after the melding. Add a large can of drained diced tomatoes at this point. If you like more tomato, have at it. Tomato sauce can be added if you like that flavor. The acidity will also tenderize the beef.

Check the chili meat for doneness in another half hour. Depending on the cut of meat you used, it could be ready. If not, check every twenty minutes for up to another hour (2.5 hours maximum cooking time).

When you are happy with the beans and the chili, mix 'em all together in a suitable pot. If the beans have not thickened to your likening, you can partially drain them before adding to the meat. If you use a crock pot, you can keep it warm for hours with no degradation in quality. For the very best chili, let the mixture cool and warm it up the next day. This is not allowed in a real chili cook-off.

Emergency fixes: If, after all this work, you have a problem, there are some last minute solutions:

My chili is too mild
Easy, add Louisiana hot sauce, chipotlé juice, even picanté sauce. Avoid raw chili powder.

My chili is too thin
Be careful with thickeners, they can turn your chili to paste. Add a little roux, a bit at a time, until it's almost thick enough. It will continue to thicken. If you don't want to make a roux, you can spoon out a half cup of the beans, puree them, and add back to the pot (repeat if necessary). If you have instant dehydrated beans, this also works.

My chili is too hot
The only hope is to increase the volume of non-spicy ingredients. Add more tomatoes or cooked beans. I've even been known to add cooked ground turkey. It's a very neutral flavor that is not often noticed by your guests.

My chili is too brown, too red, or too pale
Don't worry about it.

My chili is gone
Make more.

Tom Jones
Richmond, Kentucky
Eastern Kentucky University Colonel Fan

Bun Warmers

Home of the Card March

Burgers, Hotdogs & Sandwiches

Marcum Sideline Sloppy Joes

2 pounds hamburger, leaner the better
2 large onions, chopped
2 celery stalks, sliced thinly and chopped
1 large green pepper, chopped
1 small bottle ketchup
1 can tomato sauce or tomato soup
1 teaspoon dry mustard
1 tablespoon vinegar
1 teaspoon salt
1 tablespoon vinegar

Break up hamburger and brown thoroughly. Add onion and brown slightly. Place in deep baking dish or medium size roaster. In a small pan, make a paste of mustard and vinegar; add other ingredients and bring to a boil. Add boiling mixture to onions and hamburger. Cover and bake one hour at 400 degrees. Serve on hamburger buns or slices of thick toast.

Walter Marcum
Lancaster, Kentucky
University of Kentucky Wildcat Fan
Henry Clay High School Blue Devil Fan

Walter Marcum, Lancaster, enjoys some tailgate specials provided by Thomas and King during the University of Kentucky/University of Georgia football game in 2006. In 1952, Marcum sold hotdogs and Cokes as a boy at UK's Stoll Field and Memorial Coliseum. In 1965, Marcum began running 10 concession stands at Commonwealth Stadium until he retired in 2004. He was also a 42-year employee of the United States Postal Service. Walter is author Kelli Oakley's father.

Scorin' Burgers

1 ½ pounds lean ground beef
10¾ ounce can cheddar cheese soup
3 tablespoons green chilies, drained
½ cup dry bread crumbs
½ teaspoon salt
¼ black pepper

Fire up grill to medium heat. Mix ground beef, ½ cup cheddar cheese soup, green chilies, bread crumbs, salt, and pepper; mix well. Divide into 6 equal amounts and make 6 patties. Grill until cooked to your preference: 5 to 6 minutes on each side results in medium; 7 to 8 minutes on each side results in well done. Heat remaining cheese soup and use as sauce to top burgers.

Sean Marcum
Louisville, Kentucky
University of Florida Gator Fan

Super Bowl Sandwich Roll-Ups

Two 8-ounce packages cream cheese
1 package ranch dressing mix
Ham, chopped
Green onions, chopped
Black olives, chopped
Celery, chopped
Pecans, chopped
Green pepper, chopped
Flour tortilla shells

Mix cream cheese and ranch dressing mix. Spread evenly over tortilla shells. Spread remaining ingredients over each tortilla shell. Roll up and chill. Slice each filled tortilla shell into small rolls and serve.

Malaby Byrd
Lexington, Kentucky
University of Kentucky Wildcat Fan
Tates Creek High School Commodore Fan

Quick & Easy Barbeque

2 pounds hamburger
2 cups ketchup
4 tablespoons mustard
1 tablespoon vinegar
1 tablespoon sugar

Brown and drain hamburger. Mix together remaining ingredients.

Nikki Martin
Lexington, Kentucky
University of Kentucky Wildcat Fan

Corndog Cornbread

2 boxes Jiffy cornbread
2 hotdogs, chopped

Roll hotdogs pieces into dry mix. Prepare cornbread mix as instructed from box. Bake as instructed from box.

Russ Williams
Lexington, Kentucky
University of Kentucky Wildcat Fan

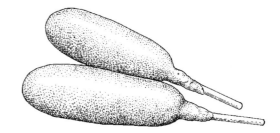

Ham Biscuits

2 sticks margarine or butter
1 small minced onion
2 teaspoons Worcestershire sauce
1½ teaspoon mustard
2 tablespoons poppy seeds

Mix all ingredients and use as filling for ham and biscuits. May add Swiss cheese and heat.

Peggy Reid
Sandston, Virginia
Virginia Tech University Hokie Fan

Cucumber Chicken Pitas

4 chicken breasts, skinless and boneless
1 cup oil
2 tablespoon Worcestershire sauce
1 cup plain yogurt
1 teaspoon celery seed
1 cucumber, peeled and cubed
1 cup sour cream
3-4 Roma tomatoes

Marinate chicken in oil and Worcestershire sauce. Grill and cut into chunks. Mix the remaining ingredients and add to grilled chicken. Spoon into pita pockets.

Kelli Oakley
Lexington, Kentucky
Henry Clay High School Blue Devil Fan
Murray State University Racer Fan

All-American Burgers

2 pounds ground beef
2 teaspoons Dijon mustard
¼ teaspoon hot sauce
1 garlic clove, minced
1 teaspoon salt
½ teaspoon pepper

Sauce:
½ cup light mayo-style salad dressing
¼ cup relish
¼ cup creamy French dressing
1 teaspoon sugar
⅓ teaspoon pepper

Mix ground beef with patty ingredients and form into 10 patties. Grill over hot coals 4 to 6 minutes on each side. Dress with your favorite condiments and spread with the special sauce. Relish the afternoon. Serves 10.

Deborah I. Back
Lexington, Kentucky
Paul Laurence Dunbar High School Bulldog Fan
University of Kentucky Wildcat Fan

Apricot Turkey Sandwiches

**3 cups cooked turkey breast, finely
     chopped**
½ cup thinly sliced celery
¾ cup mayonnaise**
¼ cup plain low-fat yogurt (optional)
4 dried apricots, chopped
2 green onions, chopped
¼ cup cashews, chopped
8 lettuce leaves
**16 slices of pumpernickel bread or bread
     of your choice**

Mix all the ingredients, except the bread and lettuce, in a bowl. Season to taste. Divide equally to make 8 sandwiches on pumpernickel bread, each with a lettuce leaf. You may cut the mayonnaise to a half of cup if you decide to use the yogurt

**Sandy Hilen
Lexington, Kentucky
University of Kentucky Wildcat Fan**

Heating Up the Gridiron

Steaks, Ribs & Other Main Dishes

Easy Grilled Shrimp

Bamboo skewers
Medium shrimp, 21/25 count
Melted butter

Cajun Spice Blend:
1½ ounce hot Hungarian paprika
½ ounce kosher salt
2 tablespoons onion powder
2 tablespoons garlic powder
2 tablespoons cayenne
1 tablespoon ground white pepper
1 tablespoon ground black pepper
1 tablespoon dried thyme
1 tablespoon dried oregano

Mix ingredients for Cajun Spice Blend. You may find it to be more potent than you care for, so adjust it accordingly. Soak skewers in cold water for an hour. Peel and de-vein the shrimp. Melt butter on low heat. Skewer shrimp from thick side through thin side and allow a space between shrimp for even cooking (4 shrimp should be plenty). Brush one side with the butter and evenly sprinkle on the seasoning. Turn over and repeat butter and seasoning. Tip: These can be made up the day before or on the spot. Grill quickly, both sides, on a hot fire. Be careful not to over cook!

Chef David Walls
Frankfort, Kentucky
New York Giant Fan

Wildcat Pork Chop Casserole

4 center cut pork chops
2 cans cream of celery soup
1 can cut or French green beans, drained
4-6 medium potatoes, peeled and sliced
1 medium onion, sliced
Salt and pepper to taste

Spread out potatoes in bottom of dish. Layer half of the onions. Spread ½ can of soup over the onion and potatoes. Spread out green beans and rest of onions. Spread ½ can of soup over mixture. Place pork chops on top and salt and pepper to taste. Spread remaining soup over pork chops. Cover and bake at 325 degrees for 1 hour and 45 minutes. Remove cover and cook 15 minutes longer.

Louise Swinford Wieman
Lexington, Kentucky
University of Kentucky Wildcat Fan

Rotini Skillet Super Bowl Dinner

1 pound hamburger
4 ounces chopped onion
16 ounces rotini pasta
1 cup cottage cheese
One 32-ounce Ragu spaghetti sauce
4 ounces mushrooms
One 12-ounce mozzarella cheese

Brown hamburger and onion in skillet. Cook rotini according to directions. In an electric skillet, spray with no-stick oil, layer half the noodles, half hamburger, half sauce and all the cottage cheese. Layer the remaining noodles, hamburger, sauce and all the mozzarella cheese. Cover and cook on low until cheese melts.

Steve Leffler
Elizabeth, Indiana
Indiana University Hoosier Fan

Bob Grossman, left, and Dan Davis waited for fans to arrive at Papa John Stadium during a University of Louisville football game in 2006. Grossman, a first year member, and Davis, a two-year member, are part of the Cardinal Club helping out during the season.

Sweet and Spicy Pork Marinade

½ stick of butter
1 small onion, chopped
2 cloves garlic, minced
¼ cup brown sugar
3 tablespoons rice vinegar
1 tablespoon hot chili oil
1 teaspoon red pepper flakes
1 tablespoon ground cumin
1 tablespoon Worcestershire sauce
2 teaspoons Dijon mustard or deli mustard
1 cup ketchup
1 cup beef broth/stock
Salt and pepper to taste
Lime juice (optional)

Sauté onion and garlic until tender. Add brown sugar and rice vinegar to the hot pan. Stir in the remaining ingredients and simmer for approximately 15 minutes. Stir occasionally. Add salt and pepper as needed. If you like a little citrus flavor, add a splash of lime juice or squeeze half of a fresh lime. Cool for 15 minutes and place in a jar if not using immediately.

Eli Brainard, a student from Somerset, Kentucky, was "official cook" for the Western Kentucky University Baptist Student Union during 2004 homecoming.

Matt Skaggs
Lexington, Kentucky
University of Kentucky Wildcat Fan

Vegetable Pizza

2 cans crescent rolls
Two 8-ounce package cream cheese
I package ranch dressing mix
Fresh green beans, chopped
Broccoli, chopped
Carrots, chopped
Shredded cheese

Lay crescent rolls on cookie sheet flat and bake at oven temperature required in directions. Cool crust. Mix cream cheese and ranch dressing mix. Spread cream cheese mixture on cooled crust. Spread green beans, broccoli, and carrots evenly on crust. Sprinkle with cheese and chill. Cut into squares and serve.

Ida Byrd
Lexington, Kentucky
University of Kentucky Wildcat Fan
Tates Creek High School Commodore Fan

BBQ Spice Mix

I ounce hot Hungarian paprika
2 tablespoons chili powder
I ¼ ounce salt
4 teaspoons ground cumin
½ ounce sugar
I tablespoon dried thyme
2 teaspoons dry mustard
2 teaspoons ground black pepper
2 teaspoons dried oregano
2 teaspoons curry powder
I teaspoon cayenne

Combine all ingredients and store in an airtight container in a cool dark place. Personally I store this and any aromatic in the freezer. If you do not have a scale to weigh the ounces, keep in mind that I tablespoon is approximately a half ounce.

David Walls
Frankfort, Kentucky
New York Giant Fan

Pineapple Ham Kabobs

6 to 8 wooden or metal skewers
1 pound ham steak, cut into 1-inch cubes
20-ounce can pineapple chunks, drained,
     with ⅔ cup juice reserved
2 large red or green bell peppers, cut into
     1-inch squares
½ cup brown sugar

Soak wooden skewers in water for 15 to 20 minutes. On each skewer, alternately thread chunks of ham, pineapple, and bell pepper. Place skewers in a 9 by 11 baking dish. In a medium glass bowl, combine pineapple juice and the brown sugar; stir until the sugar dissolves. Pour mixture over kabobs, cover, and refrigerate for about 30 minutes. Turn occasionally. Fire up grill to medium heat. Grill kabobs 9 to 12 minutes, basting with the excess marinade.

Jayna Oakley
Lexington, Kentucky
University of Kentucky Wildcat Fan
Henry Clay High School Blue Devil Fan
Lafayette High School Lady General Fan

Susie Oder, Frankfort, left, was recipient of a Wildcat quilt raffled during the RV Roadcat's fundraiser. Michele Ledington, Louisville, right, made the quilt for the raffle.

Patsy Todd's Chuck Roast Barbecue

1 (2 ½ pounds) boneless chuck roast,
    trimmed
2 small onions, chopped
1-12 ounce can cola-flavored beverage (1½
    cups)
⅓ cup Worcestershire sauce
1½ tablespoons apple cider vinegar or
    white vinegar
1½ teaspoons beef bouillon granules
¾ teaspoon dry mustard
¾ teaspoon chili powder
¼ to ½ teaspoon ground red pepper
3 garlic cloves, minced
1 cup ketchup
1 tablespoon butter or margarine

Place roast in a 3½-quart electric slow cooker. Add onion. Combine cola and next 7 ingredients. Cover and chill 1 cup sauce. Pour remaining sauce over roast. Cover and cook on high for 6 hours or on low for 9 hours or until roast is very tender. Remove roast with chopped onion from cooker, using a slotted spoon and shred meat with two forks. Combine reserved sauce, ketchup and butter in a saucepan. Cook over medium heat, stirring constantly until thoroughly heated. Pour sauce over shredded meat, stirring gently. Spoon meat mixture onto buns. Serves 6.

Patsy Todd
Lexington, Kentucky
University of Kentucky Wildcat Fan

Scorchin' Chicken Barbecue

½ cup A1 sauce
½ cup tomato sauce
¼ cup onion, chopped finely
2 teaspoons cider vinegar
2 teaspoons maple syrup
1 teaspoon vegetable oil
3 teaspoons chili powder
½ teaspoon crushed red pepper flakes
3 pound chicken, cut up

In a medium saucepan, combine steak sauce, tomato sauce, onion, vinegar, maple syrup, oil, chili powder, and red pepper flakes. Over medium heat, heat to a boil; reduce heat. Simmer 5 to 7 minutes or until thickened. Cool. Grill chicken over medium heat 30 to 40 minutes or until done, turning and basting frequently with prepared sauce.

Rodney Oakley
Lexington, Kentucky
University of Kentucky Wildcat Fan
Lafayette High School Lady General Fan

The University of Kentucky RV Roadcat Club does a potluck breakfast or lunch, depending on game-time, for every game they attend.

Leffler Chicken and Dumplings

1 whole fryer chicken
1 cup flour
Pinch salt
1 egg, large or jumbo
½ egg shell of cold water (add more if needed)

Cook chicken to make broth. If you need more broth, only use the natural with no preservatives. Season while cooking. You will need 6 quarts of broth to do the dumpling recipe 4 to 5 times. Sift flour and salt together. Mix with egg and water to form dough. Sprinkle dough and rolling surface with flour. Roll dough to ¼ inch thick. Using a pizza cutter, cut into 1-inch squares. Drop into boiling broth. Make sure you strain broth and de-bone chicken before adding dumplings. I like to reduce the heat and cook for 2 (or more) hours before serving. May season to taste with kosher salt, ground black pepper, and seasoned salt.

Steve Leffler
Elizabeth, Indiana
Indiana University Hoosier Fan

All Purpose BBQ Rub

¼ cup sugar
¼ cup brown sugar
½ cup paprika, sweet
4 tablespoons black pepper, ground course
4 tablespoons kosher salt
3 teaspoons garlic powder
3 teaspoons onion powder
1 teaspoon celery seed
2 teaspoons cayenne pepper
2 teaspoons sage, dried rub

Blend ingredients. Simple rub for meat to be cooked with the spice and allow to rest at a room temperature for 2-4 hours before cooking. Either smoke, grill, or roast.

Chef David Dodd
Floyd Knobs, Indiana
Chicago Bears Fan

Chicken Casserole

2 cups diced chicken
2 cups diced celery
½ cup toasted slivered almonds
1 cup mayonnaise
½ teaspoon salt
2 teaspoons grated onion
1 can mushroom soup
Ritz crackers or potato chips, crushed

Mix all ingredients together and put potato chips or Ritz crackers on top. Bake 30 minutes at 350 degrees. Serves 8 to 10.

Linda Herrington
Lexington, Kentucky
University of Kentucky Wildcat Fan

Breakfast Casserole

1 pound sausage
3 eggs
1½ cups milk
2 cups cheddar cheese
2 cups bread crumbs

Brown sausage and drain. Mix eggs and milk together. Grease casserole dish. Stir eggs, milk, bread and sausage and salt lightly. Stir in half of the cheese and cover with remaining cheese. Bake at 350 degrees for 60 to 70 minutes.

Carol Ann Maupin
Lexington, Kentucky
University of Kentucky Wildcat Fan

BBQ Asian Short Ribs

6 pounds beef short ribs, cut about ¼"
        thick
2 teaspoons ground sesame seeds
2 teaspoons red wine
2 teaspoons honey
2 teaspoons sesame oil
2 teaspoons water
2 teaspoons red chili flakes
2 teaspoons fresh ginger, grated
8 garlic cloves, smashed
1 cup of scallions, green and whites
1 cup of soy sauce

Mix all the ingredients together and pour over the short ribs. Let the ribs marinade overnight and turn every so often. Grill over medium-high heat until grill marks appear. It doesn't take long. Garnish with additional sesame and chopped scallions.

Jerry Hibbard
Lexington, Kentucky
University of Kentucky Wildcat Fan

Kentucky Hot Brown

1 tablespoon flour
½ stick butter
2 cups milk
½ pound Velveeta cheese
4 ounces sharp cheddar cheese
6 slices lightly toasted bread
6 slices baked turkey breast
6 slices baked ham (optional)
8 slices fried bacon
12 slices tomatoes
Cayenne pepper

Melt butter in double boiler. Add flour and stir until no lumps. Add milk; slowly add all cheeses. Cook until it reaches a thick consistency. In 9" x 13" buttered casserole dish, lay lightly toasted bread and add slice of turkey and ham on each. Pour melted cheese sauce over entire casserole. Sprinkle with cayenne pepper to desired taste. Lay bacon over top of each slice of bread. Add tomatoes to each. Broil in oven till cheese browns. Serves 6 people.

Robert Gray
Lexington, Kentucky
University of Tennessee Volunteer Fan
Henry Clay High School Blue Devil Fan

Big Red, the Western Kentucky University Hilltopper's mascot, points at photographers during the 2005 homecoming game. Big Red was celebrating his 25th birthday!

Believe It Or Not Pork Chops

6-8 pork chops
1 cup ketchup
1 cup Coke

Brown chops and place in a baking dish. Mix Coke and ketchup. Pour mixture over pork chops. Cover with foil. Bake at 375 degrees for 45 minutes.

Amy McGuire
Georgetown, Kentucky
Scott County High School Cardinal Fan

Sausage Pie

1 pound of sage sausage
16-ounce sliced mushrooms (optional)
2 eggs
12 ounces of shredded cheese (I use
	cheddar and mozzarella mix)
1 frozen pie shell (I use Pet Ritz)

Pre-heat oven 400 degrees. Brown sausage and drain. In a large mixing bowl, mix all of the ingredients together. Mix well! Pour into pie shell. If you want, you can sprinkle a little cheese on top. Bake 45 minutes. This is easy to make! I usually make 2 at a time!

Linda Bramham
Georgetown, Kentucky
Scott County High School Cardinal Fan

Bacon and Eggs Casserole

4 bacon strips
18 eggs
1 cup milk
1 cup shredded cheddar cheese
1 cup sour cream
¼ cup sliced green onions
1 to 1½ teaspoons salt
½ teaspoon pepper

In a skillet over medium heat, cook bacon until crisp, then drain. In a large bowl, beat eggs. Add milk, cheese, sour cream, onions, salt, and pepper. Pour into greased 3-quart baking dish. Crumble bacon and sprinkle on top. Bake, uncovered, at 325 degrees for 40 to 45 minutes or until a knife inserted near the center comes out clean. Let stand for 5 minutes. Makes 8-10 servings.

Sharon Hawkins
Georgetown, Kentucky
Scott County High School Cardinal Fan

Kelly Freeman used to be a "Topperette" for Western Kentucky University for two years before turning in her dancing equipment to complete her nursing degree requirements. Freeman, from Owensboro, said her school work wouldn't allow her time to be part of the dance team but she was still able to attend games, play a few Corn Holes on Saturdays and enjoy just hanging out and being with everyone. Freeman is the daughter of Brenda and Clayton Solise, Crofton, Kentucky.

Hamburger Steaks

1 pound lean ground beef
2 cans beef gravy
Salt and pepper to taste

Pad out the hamburger into 4 patties. Place patties in an 8x8 baking dish and top with 2 cans beef gravy. Top with salt and pepper. Bake at 350 degrees for one hour.

Holly Lynn
Lexington, Kentucky
University of Kentucky Wildcat Fan

Reuben Casserole

2 cans sauerkraut
1 can corned beef
½ cup Thousand Island dressing
3 tablespoons Dijon mustard
Sliced Swiss cheese
Rye bread cubes

Mix all ingredients. Bake at 350 degrees for 40 minutes.

Peggy Reid
Sandston, Virginia
Virginia Tech University Hokie Fan

During a 2006 game at Commonwealth Stadium, the Winke tailgaters braved the cool temperatures. The group included, left to right, Don Cooper, Karen Cooper, Andy Weiner, Joy Weiner, Pat Winke and Linda Winke.

Dee's Mexican Chicken Casserole

6-8 cooked and diced boneless/skinless
    chicken breasts
2 cups cooked rice
3 tomatoes, chopped
2 large onions, chopped
2 cans green chilies
2 tablespoons garlic, minced
1 can cream of chicken soup condensed
16-ounce container of cottage cheese
16-ounce container of sour cream
1 pound shredded monetary jack cheese
16 ounces cream cheese, softened and
    cubed
1 package of taco seasoning
Jalapenos (optional)
Salt and pepper to taste
1 bag of crushed Fritos

Cook and chop chicken. Place in a very large bowl. Combine all the cheeses with the sour cream, undiluted soup, taco seasoning, garlic, chilies, onion, and tomatoes. Cook rice and add hot rice to mixture in the bowl. It makes the cheese blend easier. Blend well and place in a large baking dish. You can add jalapenos into the mix or place on top of mixture after putting in baking dish. Take crushed Fritos and sprinkle over the top. Bake at 450 degrees until hot and bubbly, approximately 30 to 45 minutes.

Dee McIntosh
Georgetown, Kentucky
Scott County High School Cardinal Fan

Lemon-Curry Chicken Casserole

Two 12-ounce packages frozen cut
    asparagus, thawed and drained
4 boneless chicken breasts, cut into ½-inch
    strips
Salt and pepper to taste
3 tablespoons butter or margarine
1 can cream of chicken soup, undiluted
½ cup mayonnaise
¼ cup lemon juice
1 teaspoon curry powder
¼ teaspoon ground ginger
⅛ teaspoon pepper
½ cup sliced almonds, toasted

Place asparagus in a greased 11x7x2 baking dish.
Sprinkle chicken with salt and pepper. In large skillet,
sauté chicken in butter for 10-14 minutes. Place over
asparagus. Combine soup, mayonnaise, lemon juice,
curry powder, ginger and pepper. Spoon over
chicken. Bake uncovered at 350 degrees for 35
minutes. Sprinkle with almonds and return to over
for another 5 minutes.

Peggy Reid
Sandston, Virginia
Virginia Tech University Hokie Fan

*Brandon Hostettler, Nashville, TN, watches closely
as his opponent, right, Chris Handlon, Evansville, IN,
takes his turn throwing during a corn hole game at a
Western Kentucky University homecoming football
game.*

Chicken Casserole

5-6 chicken breasts
1 stick butter
1 can cream of celery soup
1 can cream of onion soup
1 cup sour cream
1½ to 2 cups chicken broth
1 box Stove Top dressing

Cook chicken, take out bone, cut in bite-size pieces. Melt butter and drizzle over chicken. Mix soups and sour cream, pour over chicken, top with Stove Top dressing. Pour chicken broth over chicken and dressing. Cover and bake for 30 minutes on 350 degrees. Uncover and bake 15 minutes to brown.

Joe Wayne Charles
Georgetown, Kentucky
University of Kentucky Wildcat Fan
Scott County High School Cardinal Fan

Mexican Chicken

2 cans chunk chicken breast
2 cans green enchilada sauce
8 ounces cream cheese
1 small can green chilies
10 flour tortillas
1 package of pepper jack cheese or
     cheddar cheese

Cube cream cheese. Brown chicken and shred. Add cream cheese and green chilies and stir until it melts. Put two tablespoons in each flour tortilla and roll up, placing in 9 x 13 casserole dish with seam side down. Pour enchilada sauce over this and top with shredded pepper jack cheese or cheddar cheese. Bake at 400 degrees for 15 minutes.

Peggy Reid
Sandston, Virginia
Virginia Tech University Hokie Fan

Tortilla Wrap Roll-Up

1 tortilla wrap
4-ounce package of cream cheese,
    softened
1 scallion, thinly sliced, or medium onion,
    finely diced
1 small green pepper, finely diced
3 baby carrots, finely sliced

Lay wrap out flat. Spread cream cheese over entire wrap. Lay scallion (or sprinkle onion) over cream cheese. Sprinkle green pepper and carrots. Roll up jellyroll style and chill overnight. Slice into ½-inch thick pieces. Note: May also add red pepper, shredded lettuce, sliced olives, and hot peppers to wrap.

Robert Koegel
Lexington, Kentucky

Asian Pork Tenderloin

1½ pound pork tenderloin
2 tablespoons soy sauce
2 tablespoons sesame oil
2 tablespoons brown sugar, packed
1 tablespoon Worcestershire sauce
1 tablespoon lemon juice
2 cloves garlic, crushed
½ tablespoon dry mustard
¾ teaspoon pepper

Wisk together first eight ingredients. Marinate pork in this for up to eight hours in the refrigerator. Remove pork from marinade and discard marinade. Place in a foil-lined roasting pan. Bake at 350 degrees for 25 minutes or until pork reaches an internal temperature of 160 degrees.

Peggy Reid
Sandston, Virginia
Virginia Tech University Hokie Fan

Spicy Shrimp and Pasta Casserole

2 eggs
1½ cups half-and-half
1 cup plain yogurt
½ cup grated Swiss cheese
⅓ cup crumbled feta cheese
⅓ cup chopped fresh parsley leaves
1 teaspoon dried basil, crushed
1 teaspoon dried oregano, crushed
9 ounces angel hair pasta, cooked
16 ounces mild salsa, thick and chunky
2 pounds shrimp, cleaned, peeled, and
    de-veined
½ cup grated Monterey Jack

Preheat the oven to 350 degrees. Grease a 12 by 8 inch pan or glass dish with butter. Combine the eggs, half-and-half, yogurt, Swiss and feta cheeses, parsley, basil, and oregano in a large bowl, mixing until thoroughly blended. Spread ½ of the cooked pasta evenly over the bottom of the prepared pan. Cover the pasta with the salsa. Add ½ of the shrimp and then cover it with Monterey Jack. Add the remaining pasta and shrimp. Spread the egg mixture over top of the casserole. Bake for 30 minutes or until bubbly. Let stand for 10 minutes before serving.

Peggy Reid
Sandston, Virginia
Virginia Tech University Hokie Fan

Grilled Beef Tenderloin

1 – 5 to 6 pound beef tenderloin,
    trimmed & sliced into steaks
5 green onions, finely chopped
1 cup soy sauce
1 cup dry sherry
2 teaspoons olive oil

Stir together sherry, soy sauce and green onions. Rub steaks with olive oil. Put into a deep dish and then pour sherry mixture over steaks and marinate overnight. Grill over hot coals.

Sandy Hilen
Lexington, Kentucky
University of Kentucky Wildcat Fan

Crab Quiche

1 pie crust
½ cup mayonnaise
2 tablespoons flour
2 large eggs, beaten
½ cup half-and-half
6 ounces of lump crabmeat, drained
½ pound swiss cheese, grated
⅓ cup chopped green onions
Dash of Old Bay seasoning
Dash of salt

Bake pie crust at 400 degrees until lightly browned. Mix Old Bay seasoning, salt, and flour. Add mix to cheese. Beat eggs, milk and mayonnaise together. Combine with onion and crab meat. Add to pie crust and bake at 350 degrees for 30 to 40 minutes until firm.

Peggy Reid
Sandston, Virginia
Virginia Tech University Hokie Fan

Barbecued Meat Loaf

2 pounds ground beef
1 cup dry bread crumbs or cracker crumbs
1 medium onion, finely chopped
1 egg, beaten
4 tablespoons catsup
½ cup whole milk
1 teaspoon salt
¼ teaspoon pepper
8 tablespoons vinegar
8 tablespoons dark brown sugar
4 tablespoons Worcestershire sauce
1 cup catsup
½ cup chopped onion

Combine beef, breadcrumbs, onion, egg, catsup, milk, salt, and pepper. Blend well and shape into one large loaf or 4 individual loaves. In a saucepan, combine the remaining ingredients and bring to a boil. Lower heat and simmer for 5 minutes. Pour over top of meat loaf. Bake meat loaf in a 350 degrees oven for 50 to 60 minutes.

Linda Herrington
Lexington, Kentucky
University of Kentucky Wildcat Fan

Brooks Downing, third from left, former sports information director at the University of Kentucky, poses with friends and family during a University of Kentucky football game. Left to right, back row, is Alex Nugent, Lea Nugent, Brooks Downing, Cassie Downing, Robyn Hayes, Bobby Hayes, Cathy Corales, Romy Corales, front row -- left to right, Kelly Corales, Robby Hayes, Laura Hayes and Katelyn Corales.

"Put me in, Coach!" Chicken Breasts

4 skinless boneless chicken breast halves
½ container Bluegrass Winning Spread
⅓ cup shredded fresh flat leaf parsley
       leaves
1 teaspoon grated lemon zest
¾ teaspoon salt
⅓ cup toasted pecans
2 tablespoons plain dried breadcrumbs
4 teaspoons olive oil
3 tablespoons flour
½ cup white wine
1 cup chicken broth
3 tablespoons fresh lemon juice

With sharp chef's knife, make a pocket in each chicken breast half. In food processor, combine Bluegrass Winning Spread, parsley, lemon zest, and ¼ teaspoon salt. Process until smooth. Add toasted pecans and breadcrumbs and process until coarsely chopped. Sprinkle remaining ½ teaspoon salt inside pockets and on outsides of chicken breasts. Spoon mixture into pockets and secure with toothpicks. In large nonstick skillet, heat oil over medium heat. Dredge chicken in flour, shaking off excess. Add chicken to skillet and sauté, turning chicken over as it browns, about 15 minutes or until richly browned and almost cooked through. Remove to oven proof baking dish and place in warm oven.

Add wine to pan and simmer over medium heat until you have about 2 tablespoons remaining. Add broth and lemon juice and bring to a boil. Turn heat down, cover and return chicken to pan, cooking an additional 7 minutes or until chicken is cooked through. Remove toothpicks from chicken. Serve chicken with sauce spooned over meat. Garnish with parsley and serve.

Blanca Mikell Ward
Lexington, Kentucky
University of Kentucky Wildcat Fan

Hot Brown Casserole

1½ - 2 pounds ham
1½ - 2 pounds turkey
1 pound bacon
9-10 slices bread
1½ cups butter
1½ cup all purpose flour
1½ quarts milk
1-3 medium tomatoes cubed
1½ teaspoon salt
⅓ teaspoon white pepper
1½ - 2 cups Parmesan cheese

Fry bacon, drain well, cool and crumble. Set aside. Cut ham and turkey into bite size and set aside. Cube bread and put in single layer on cookie sheet. Melt butter and pour over bread. Toast in oven at 450 degrees until brown and crisp. Turn frequently. Line 9 x 13 dish with toasted crumbs. Add ham and turkey. Prepare sauce in heavy pan – melt butter, gradually add flour until thick consistency. In another pan bring milk to just below a boil then stir in flour and butter. Mix with a mixer or wisk, then stir in Parmesan cheese. Pour over ham and turkey. Cover top with cheddar cheese and extra Parmesan cheese. Cook in 350-degree oven until bubbly. Take out of oven and add tomatoes and bacon. Place under broiler until brown.

Laura Hayes
Lexington, Kentucky
University of Kentucky Wildcat Fan

Stuffed Shells

1 box large or jumbo shells, cooked and
drained
1 large carton small curd cottage cheese
8 ounces cream cheese, softened
1 box frozen chopped spinach, thawed &
drained
2 cups or so of shredded mozzarella &
provolone
½ cup grated cheese
1 egg beaten
Oregano
Pinch of salt
Classico tomato and basil sauce

When Dawn Eads tailgates, so does Lexie, her
eight-year-old Jack Russell. Lexie likes to wear her
University of Kentucky sweater to show support for
the Wildcats!

Mix cottage cheese, spinach, cheeses, eggs and
seasonings. Break cream cheese into chunks and mix
well with cottage cheese mixture. Cover bottom of
9x13 pans with tomato sauce. Stuff shells and put
into pan as one layer. Cover with tomato sauce and
grated cheese. Cover with foil and bake at 350
degrees for about 35-40 minutes. Uncover and let
rest for a minute or so. If made ahead and
refrigerated, cook for about 50-55 minutes or until
hot.

Ann Gaudinier
Lexington, Kentucky
University of Kentucky Wildcat Fan

Grilled Orange Pork Tenderloin

Whole pork tenderloin, cut into steaks,
    1 to 1¾ inches
¾ cup orange juice
1-2 teaspoons of chopped ginger
¾ cup soy sauce
2 to 3 tablespoons lemon juice
2 tablespoons olive oil
¾ cup soy sauce
2-3 tablespoons lemon juice
2 tablespoons olive oil

Mix together orange juice, soy sauce, lemon juice, olive oil and ginger. Marinade meat in ziplock bag with orange juice mixture for 3-4 hours or overnight. Grill over hot coals or bake at 350 degrees.

Jordan Baker
Lexington, Kentucky
University of Kentucky Wildcat Fan

Shrimp Bake

½ pound fresh mushrooms
4 tablespoons butter
2 cups cleaned, cooked shrimp
2 cups cooked rice
1 cup chopped green & red pepper
1 cup chopped green onion
1 cup celery, chopped
½ cup pimento, chopped
One 20-ounce can diced tomatoes, drained
¾ teaspoon salt
½ teaspoon chili powder
½ cup butter, melted

Sauté mushrooms in 4 tablespoons of butter. Combine mushrooms with rest of ingredients. Bake in 350-degree oven for 15 – 20 minutes. Serves 6-8.

Robyn Hayes
Lexington, Kentucky
University of Kentucky Wildcat Fan

Cheatin' Chicken

4 boneless skinless chicken breasts
One 16-ounce jar of salsa
Tortilla chips
Shredded Mexican blend cheese
2 cans green sauce
2 cans red sauce
Taco seasoning
Sour cream
Tomatoes, diced

Cook chicken very slow until tender enough to shred with fingers. Mix chicken, ½ jar of salsa, ½ pack of taco seasoning, ½ bag of shredded cheese and 1½ cans of red sauce. Spoon mixture into tortilla and fold. Place seam side down in casserole dish. Cover with remainder of cheese and cover with 2 cans of green sauce. Bake at 350 degrees until cheese is bubbly. Garnish with sour cream and diced tomatoes.

Jayna Oakley
Lexington, Kentucky
University of Kentucky Wildcat Fan
Henry Clay Blue Devil Fan
Lafayette High School Lady General Fan

Off-Sides

Veggies, 'Taters
& Other Side Dishes

Baked Beans Worthy of a Touchdown

2 cans baked beans
1 can apple pie filling
1 pound hot sausage
⅓ cup steak sauce
⅓ cup barbeque sauce
½ cup molasses
1 teaspoon hot sauce

Brown sausage and drain off grease. Add sausage to all other ingredients. Mix well. Pour into casserole. Bake uncovered at 350 degrees for one hour.

SK Zimmerman
Simpsonville, Kentucky

Friend Greg Allnut and Charlie Graviss sample some of the famous Graviss seafood gumbo during a Western Kentucky University Hilltopper tailgate party.

Best in the SEC Barbecue Bean Bake

1 pound ground beef
1 pound bacon, chopped
1 onion, chopped
½ cup ketchup
½ cup barbecue sauce
1 teaspoon salt
1 teaspoon chili powder
4 tablespoons prepared mustard
¾ teaspoon pepper
Two 16-ounce cans red kidney beans
Two 16-ounce cans pork and beans
Two 16-ounce cans butter beans
Brown sugar, optional

Brown ground beef, bacon and onion. Drain excess fat. Combine and add all other ingredients except the beans; stir well. Add beans and combine thoroughly. Bake for 1 hour at 350 degrees. Serves 20.

Gene Oakley
Lexington, Kentucky
University of Kentucky Wildcat Fan
Henry Clay High School Blue Devil Fan

Bourbon Sweet Potatoes with Pineapple

3 cups canned sweet potatoes, mashed
½ stick butter, melted
1 cup brown sugar
½ cup crushed pineapple, drained
⅛ cup Kentucky bourbon
¾ cup granulated sugar
½ cup self-rising flour
½ stick butter
½ cup chopped pecans

Combine the sweet potatoes with the melted butter, add the sugar and pineapple; mix well. Pour in the bourbon and stir well. Spoon the mixture into a greased, two-quart casserole dish. Mix together sugar and self-rising flour. Cut in the butter with a pastry blender until mixture looks like little peas. Add chopped pecans and mix, then sprinkle on top of potatoes. Bake at 350 degrees for 30 to 45 minutes.

Jennifer Barlow
Owensboro, Kentucky
University of Kentucky Wildcat Fan

Best Ever Potatoes

7 cups red potatoes, coarsely chopped, small
1 cup onion, chopped
8-ounce carton sour cream
1 cup shredded Monterey Jack cheese
1 cup shredded sharp cheddar cheese
½ teaspoon salt
¼ teaspoon cayenne pepper
2 medium tomatoes, chopped

Cook potatoes and onion in a large covered saucepan for 12 to 14 minutes or until tender; then drain. Stir in sour cream, Monterey jack cheese, cheddar cheese, salt, and cayenne pepper. Stir in tomatoes. Spoon all in a 2-quart rectangular baking dish and bake uncovered at 350 degrees for 30 minutes.

Judy Cox
Lexington, Kentucky
University of Kentucky Wildcat Fan
Paris High School Lady Hound Fan

Nathan Sturtzel, left, and cousin Josh Payton, both of Louisville, played cornhole during the University of Louisville/West Virginia football game on Nov. 2, 2006. Payton said he has been tailgating at Cardinal games since he was six years old and that his cousin Nathan was tailgating long before he was born! The boys' grandfather, Gil Sturtzel, is a University of Louisville Hall of Fame football player and was captain of UofL's first bowl team in the Sun Bowl.

Cheesy Potatoes

4 potatoes cut into bite size cubes
1 package Stouffer's Welsh Rarebit
    Creamy Cheddar Cheese Sauce

Boil potatoes until tender. Microwave sauce according to package directions and pour over potatoes. Stir and serve. Serves about 4 people.

Holly Lynn
Lexington, Kentucky
University of Kentucky Wildcat Fan

Matt Combs, Sal's Chop House, Lexington, showed off the feast he was preparing during the University of Kentucky/University of Georgia game. He cooked 120 pounds of wings and 80 pounds of ribs.

Potato Casserole

2 pounds frozen cubed potatoes
10¾-ounce can cream chicken soup
8 ounces sour cream
1 medium onion, chopped
16 ounces shredded cheese

Topping:
1 stick of butter
2 cups cornflakes, crushed

Mix all ingredients in a 9 x 13 casserole dish. Melt butter and mix with crushed cornflakes for topping. Bake at 350 degrees for 45 minutes.

Beth Oakley
Lexington, Kentucky
University of Kentucky Wildcat Fan
Lafayette High School Lady General Fan

Pineapple Casserole

1 large can of crushed pineapple,
        do not drain
3 eggs
1 stick butter, softened
6 slices white bread, toasted and cubed
1 teaspoon vanilla
½ teaspoon salt
1 cup sugar

Mix all ingredients except pineapple and bread cubes. When mixed, add to pineapple and mix gently. Add the bread last and pour into greased casserole dish. Bake uncovered at 350 degrees for 50 to 55 minutes.

Kelly Zimmerman
Simpsonville, Kentucky

Garlic and Herb Potatoes

1 small bag of new potatoes
2 tbsp. extra virgin olive oil
2 cloves of garlic
1 tbsp. parsley flakes
Pinch of salt
Pinch of pepper
1 tablespoon Italian seasoning

Cut potatoes into uniform bite-size pieces. Put oil and herbs in plastic bag, add potatoes and shake. Pour potatoes into a greased casserole dish and bake at 350 degrees for about 45 minutes.

Holly Lynn
Lexington, Kentucky
University of Kentucky Wildcat Fan

Long Bomb Broccoli Casserole

1 family-sized bag frozen broccoli, chopped
1½ sticks butter
4 tablespoons all-purpose flour
1 cup chicken bullion
2 cups milk
1½ pounds Velveeta cheese
2 sleeves Ritz crackers, crumbled
1 stick butter

Steam broccoli. Melt butter in medium sauce pan. Stir in flour until creamy. Add milk and bullion. Stir until mixture reaches thick consistency (if needed, add 1 more tablespoon flour). Gradually add cheese and cook until completely melted. Pour drained broccoli into 9 inch x 13 inch casserole dish. Pour cheese sauce over broccoli. In medium glass bowl, melt 1 stick butter and add crumbled crackers, mixing well. Sprinkle cracker mixture over casserole. Bake in 350 degree oven for 15 to 20 minutes.

In Memory of Clema "Brownie" White
Lexington, Kentucky

Zucchini Casserole

1 medium zucchini, sliced
One 10¾-ounce can tomato soup
1 small onion, diced
1 small green pepper, diced
1 cup shredded American cheese
¼ cup water
½ teaspoon salt
⅛ teaspoon pepper
2 tablespoons margarine

Melt margarine in skillet, add onion and pepper; sauté till tender, add zucchini, salt, and pepper. Cook over low heat, stirring till zucchini is tender. Remove from heat, add tomato soup, stirring well, and then add water. Spoon into casserole dish and sprinkle cheese on top. Bake at 400 degrees until cheese melts.

Sylvia Jackson
Lexington, Kentucky

Marinated Asparagus

⅔ cup white vinegar
½ cup sugar
½ teaspoon salt
1 teaspoon whole cloves
3 sticks cinnamon
1 tablespoon celery seed
½ cup water
3 or 4 cans asparagus spears, drained

Mix first 7 ingredients and bring to a boil. Pour over asparagus and marinate 24 to 48 hours.

Peggy Reid
Sandston, Virginia
Virginia Tech University Hokie Fan

Lima Bean Casserole

20-ounce baby frozen lima beans
½ cup or 1 large onion, diced
3 tablespoons flour
1 cup mushrooms pieces, drained
½ cup butter or margarine
¾ cup celery, chopped
2 cups half and half (may use 1 cup of milk
      & 1 cup of half and half)

Cook baby limas according to package directions and drain. Cook onion and celery in butter (don't brown) till tender. Add flour to vegetables and milk until it thickens. Add mushrooms. May be served immediately or place in oven on 300 degrees. Sprinkle with paprika before serving.

Marie M. Brown
Anamosa, Iowa
University of Iowa Hawkeye Fan

Bill and Sandy Rader showed off a "Mountaineer Doll" their granddaughter Jennifer bought for them to take on game road trips. From Summersville, West Virginia, the Raders tailgated at the University of Louisville/West Virginia game on Nov. 2, 2006.

Jessie Mac's Squash Casserole

2 pounds yellow squash
1 medium onion
1 stick butter
2 eggs, beaten
4 slices bread, crumbled
1 to 2 cups cheddar cheese, cubed

Slice, boil and drain squash and onion. Add other ingredients, mixing well after each ingredient. Bake at 350 degrees for 30 minutes in greased baking dish. "I remember watching my grandmother prepare this dish about 25 years ago and to this day, it's still one of my favorite dishes. Kids will usually eat it if you call it cheesy casserole."

Linda Watkins
Lexington, Kentucky
University of Kentucky Wildcat Fan

Irv Schmidt, a retired Fischer's Packing Company employee, mans a caboose right across from Papa John Stadium during the University of Louisville's home games. Schmidt said he and his wife, Peggy, serve their specialty dish, grilled bologna, to 100 or so clients, friends and employees during the Cardinals home games.

Sweet Potatoes and Nuts

3 – 4 large (29½ ounce) cans sweet
    potatoes, drained and mashed
1 cup sugar
1 teaspoon vanilla
½ cup butter, melted
1 cup flour
1 cup walnuts or pecans, chopped
½ cup brown sugar
½ cup butter, melted

Combine first 4 ingredients in a baking dish. Top with last 4 ingredients. Bake at 350 degrees for 30 minutes or until golden brown.

Janie Rusch
Georgetown, Kentucky
Scott County High School Cardinal Fan

Marinated Vegetables

1 can white shoe peg corn
1 can peas
1 can French style green beans
1 cup celery, diced
½ cup onion, diced
1 large jar pimentos

Drain all vegetables. Combine the following and pour over vegetables.

1 cup sugar
1 teaspoon salt
1 teaspoon pepper
½ cup oil
¾ cup white vinegar
1 teaspoon water

Add a dash of Accent; refrigerate.

Peggy Reid
Sandston, Virginia
Virginia Tech University Hokie Fan
Baking potatoes

Packet Potatoes
Baking Potatoes
Velveeta cheese, cut into cubes
Butter
Salt and pepper
Aluminum foil

Cut up one potato into bite-size cubes and place on a sheet of aluminum foil. Add Velveeta cheese to the potato along with some butter, then add salt and pepper last. Cover with the foil to make a packet, folding at the top. Cook on a grill for about 45 minutes, checking on it occasionally. Eat directly out of the packet and enjoy!!!

Holly Lynn
Lexington, Kentucky
University of Kentucky Wildcat Fan

The UK RV Roadcat Club posed for a photo during a University of Kentucky Wildcat football game. The RV Club has around 90 RVs in the club and travel from game to game.

Broccoli Cornbread

10-ounce box frozen chopped broccoli,
   thawed and drained
2 tablespoons chopped onion
6-ounce carton small curd cottage cheese
1 stick margarine, melted
4 eggs, beaten
8½-ounce box Jiffy cornbread mix

Mix first five ingredients. Add cornbread mix. Pour into 9 x 13 pan. Bake at 400 degrees for 20-25 minutes.

Peggy Reid
Sandston, Virginia
Virginia Tech University Hokie Fan

The Western Kentucky University "Corn Hole Crew" loves Saturday tailgating! Taking time out for a photo during Homecoming 2005, left to right, is Joe Mattingly (Evansville, IN), Joey Sinnett (Evansville), Adam Nicholson (Evansville), Anthony McClellan (Carthage, TN), Chris Handlon (Evansville) and Brandon Hostettler (Nashville, TN).

Scalloped Potatoes and Sausage

1 pound smoked sausage
1 medium onion, sliced
Flour
6 medium potatoes
Salt, to taste
Pepper, to taste
Milk
Margarine

Wash, peel, and slice the potatoes very thin. Place in baking dish. Fill dish two-thirds full with layers of potato and onion slices. Sprinkle each layer with salt, pepper, flour, and dots of butter. Add milk until almost covered. Cover dish and bake at 350 degrees for 45 minutes. Remove and place sausage on top and return to oven for about 20 minutes or until sausage is done and browned.

Gloria Casey
Georgetown, Kentucky
Scott County High School Cardinal Fan

Cowboy Beans

½ pound ground beef or sausage
½ pound bacon
1 cup onion, chopped
1 can pork and beans
1 can kidney beans, drained
1 can lima beans, drained
1 can butter beans, drained
½ cup brown sugar
½ cup sugar
1 teaspoon salt
½ cup catsup
1 teaspoon dry mustard
2 tablespoons vinegar

Brown ground beef and bacon; drain. Add onions and beans. Add brown sugar, granulated sugar, salt, catsup, dry mustard, and vinegar. Put in casserole dish and bake at 350 degrees for 40 minutes.

Kim Valdez
Georgetown, Kentucky
Scott County High School Cardinal Fan

Best in the Bluegrass Potato Salad

Salad Ingredients:
4 cups water
2 pounds small new red potatoes
    (equals out to around 14)
3 cups water
½ pound fresh green beans,
    cut into 1½-inch pieces
8 ounces American cheese, cubes ½ inch
6 ounces salami, cubed ½ inch

Dressing Ingredients:
½ cup sour cream
½ cup mayonnaise
¼ cup chopped red onion
2 tablespoons country-style Dijon mustard
½ teaspoon coarsely ground pepper

In a 3-quart saucepan, bring 4 cups water to a boil and add potatoes. Cook over high heat for 12 minutes or until potatoes are fork tender. Drain and rinse with cold water. Cool and cut into ¼ inch slices. Then, bring 3 cups water to a full boil in a 2-quart saucepan; add beans. Cook over high heat for 5 minutes or until crisply tender. Drain and rinse with cold water. In a large bowl, you want to place potatoes, beans, cheese, and salami. To make the dressing, in a small bowl, stir together sour cream, mayonnaise, red onion, mustard, and pepper. Gently stir dressing into salad to coat well. Cover and refrigerate at least one hour.

Kelli Oakley
Lexington, Kentucky
Henry Clay High School Blue Devil Fan

How Sweet It Is!

Cakes, Cookies
& Other Sweet Treats

Shortbread

1 pound plain flour
½ pound margarine
2 ounces butter
6 ounces caster sugar (very fine sugar)

Rub all ingredients together and then kneed. Bake at 350 degrees for approximately 1 hour. Makes 3 cakes of shortbread. Sprinkle top with caster sugar when out of oven.

Note: If caster sugar is not available, just grind sugar down finer.

George Cowan
Edinburg, Scotland
Henry Clay High School Blue Devil Fan

Easy Peanut Brittle

1 cup sugar
½ cup light corn syrup
Dash of salt
1 to 1½ cups shelled raw peanuts
1 tablespoon margarine or butter
1½ teaspoon baking soda
1 teaspoon vanilla

Grease baking sheet heavily. Combine sugar, corn syrup and salt in 3-quart casserole. Stir in peanuts. Microwave at high until light brown, 8 to 10 minutes (stirring once or twice). Stir in remaining ingredients until light and foamy. Quickly spread on greased baking sheet. Spread as thin as possible for brittle candy. Cool; break into pieces.

Gene Oakley
Lexington, Kentucky
University of Kentucky Wildcat Fan
Henry Clay High School Blue Devil Fan
Lafayette High School Lady General Fan

Fresh Apple Cake with Caramel Glaze

¼ cup cinnamon-sugar mixture
4 apples, chopped small
3 eggs
1 cup vegetable oil
2 cups all-purpose flour
2 cups sugar
½ teaspoon baking soda
1 teaspoon cinnamon

Glaze:
2 teaspoons butter
½ cup firmly packed brown sugar
2 tablespoons milk

Preheat oven to 350 degrees. Grease a bundt or tube pan and coat with cinnamon-sugar mixture. Mix apples, eggs, and oil. Add flour, sugar, baking soda, and cinnamon; mix well. Pour into pan and bake 50 to 60 minutes or until toothpick inserted in center comes out clean. Allow cake to rest in pan at least 10 minutes. Invert onto a cake plate. Prepare glaze in medium sauce pan by bringing butter, brown sugar, and milk to a boil. Poke holes in cake with toothpick and dribble glaze over cake. Allow to cool before serving. Tip: Serve with a scoop of vanilla ice cream or Cool Whip. May also add chopped nuts to cake if desired.

Debbie Baker
Danville, Kentucky
Boyle County High School Rebel Fan
Western Kentucky University Hilltopper Fan

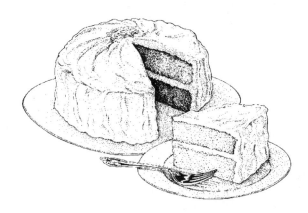

Peanut Butter and Chocolate Cheeseball

8-ounce package cream cheese, softened
¼ cup butter, softened
¼ cup creamy peanut butter
¾ cup powdered sugar
3 tablespoons unsweetened cocoa, powdered
½ cup chocolate chips
½ cup peanut butter chips
⅔ cup peanut butter 2 tbsp. Brown suger
⅔ cup pecans, finely chopped

Beat cream cheese, butter and peanut butter at a medium speed until smooth. Stir in sugars, cocoa, and chips. Cover and chill for 2 hours or until firm. Shape into a ball and roll into chopped pecans. Serve with graham crackers.

Linda Oakley
Lexington, Kentucky
University of Kentucky Wildcat Fan
Henry Clay High School Blue Devil Fan
Lafayette High School Lady General Fan

Twinkie Cake

Twinkies
1 large box vanilla pudding
2 to 3 bananas
1 large can crushed pineapple, drain
Cool Whip
1 jar maraschino cherries

Cut twinkies in half and lay in a 9 x 13 pan. Mix pudding according to directions and pour over Twinkies. Slice bananas and spread over pudding mixture. Mix pineapple and Cool Whip and place on top of bananas. Slice cherries and place on top throughout.

Allie Leffler
Louisville, Kentucky
University of Indiana Hoosier Fan

Fruit Loaf

2 teacups self-rising flour
1 teacup dried fruit
1 egg
½ teacup sugar
2 ounces margarine

Rub margarine into dry ingredients. Add fruit. Add egg and milk to make a soft consistency. Bake in a greased loaf tin for 1 hour at 400 degrees.

George Cowan
Edinburg, Scotland
Henry Clay High School Blue Devil Fan

Chocolate Bread Pudding

20 ounces heavy cream
10 ounces milk
4 ounces sugar
5 ounces bittersweet chocolate, chopped
1 ounce dark rum, optional
1 teaspoon vanilla
1 egg, beaten
10 ounces white bread, diced with crust removed

Pre-set oven at 350 degrees. Combine cream, milk, and sugar in a saucepan; heat and stir until sugar dissolves. Cool for 1 minute; then add the chocolate and dissolve. Add the vanilla with the rum. Stir to mix well. Place the diced bread in a suitable buttered hotel pan. Pour the chocolate mixture over the bread and make sure all the bread is covered and coated. Bake for approximately 30 to 45 minutes. May serve hot or cool. Serves 6.

Chef David Dodd
Floyd Knobs, Indiana
Chicago Bears Fan

Kelli Oakley interviews students from Western Kentucky University for Kentucky TALEgating II, More Stories with Sauce.

Tray Bake – Peppermint Slice

4 ounces self-rising flour
2 ounces brown sugar
4 ounces margarine
1 teaspoon baking powder
1 tablespoon drinking chocolate

Icing:
½ cup icing sugar
5 drops green colouring
½ teaspoon peppermint essence
Enough water to mix icing sugar (delicate)

Melt margarine and add all dry ingredients. Press into baking tray and bake for 20 minutes at 180 degrees. Spread icing on base while still hot. Coat with melted chocolate.

George Cowan
Edinburg, Scotland
Henry Clay High School Blue Devil Fan

Pound Cake

1 cup butter, softened
½ cup shortening
3 cups sugar
5 eggs
3 cups all-purpose flour
½ teaspoon baking powder
1 cup milk
½ teaspoon vanilla extract

Cream butter, sugar, and shortening until light and fluffy. Add eggs, one at a time, beating well after each addition. Sift together the dry ingredients. Add sifted ingredients to creamed mixture, alternating with milk and vanilla. Do not overmix. Pour batter into a greased and floured loaf pan. Bake at 325° for about 1¼ to 1½ hours, or until a wooden pick or cake tester inserted in center comes out clean.

Malaby Byrd
Lexington, Kentucky
University of Kentucky Wildcat Fan
Tates Creek High School Commodore Fan

The "Bomb" Coffee Cake

1 stick butter
1½ cups sugar
2 eggs
1 cup sour cream
1 teaspoon vanilla
2 cups flour
1½ teaspoons baking powder
1 teaspoon baking soda
1 cup nuts, pecans preferred
1 teaspoon cinnamon

Melt butter; cool. Mix with 1 cup sugar (save ½ cup for later), eggs, sour cream, and vanilla until well blended. Mix in flour combined with baking powder and soda. Pour into an 8 x 9 pan or a bundt cake pan. Mix nuts with remaining sugar and cinnamon; swirl into batter. Bake 1 hour at 350 degrees.

Kelli Oakley
Lexington, Kentucky
Henry Clay High School Blue Devil Fan
Murray State University Racer Fan

Seven Layer Cookies

1 stick butter or margarine
1 ¼ cup graham cracker crumbs
1 cup chocolate chips
1 cup butterscotch chips
1 cup coconut
1 cup chopped walnuts
1 can sweetened condensed milk

Melt butter in 13 x 9 x 2 pan. Sprinkle graham cracker crumbs over the butter. Mix with fork, then press evenly for the bottom crust. Sprinkle the next 4 ingredients in the order listed. Pat into crust. Pour sweetened condensed milk evenly to cover the entire top. Bake at 350 degrees for 30 minutes or till brown and bubbly around the edges. Cool, cut, and serve.

Mary Platt Clements
Versailles, Kentucky
University of Kentucky Wildcat Fan

When it comes to tailgating, Linda Winke and her friends and family enjoy getting together and exchanging recipes for all kinds of great dishes and drinks! From left to right, posing in front of Commonwealth Stadium, standing is Andy Weiner, Karen Cooper, Linda Winke, Eric Winke, Molly Winke, Marshall Peace and lying down, Don Cooper and Pat Winke.

Transparent Pie

2 sticks butter
2 cups sugar
1 tablespoon
Pinch of salt
½ can Carnation milk
3 eggs, slightly beaten
1 tablespoon vanilla
1 teaspoon lemon extract

Using a double-broiler pan, cream butter and sugar. Add eggs and remaining ingredients. Heat until butter is melted and sugar is dissolved. Pour into an unbaked pie crust or one dozen small tarts. Bake at 400 degrees for 10 minutes, then reduce oven to 350 degrees and cook until brown on top.

In Memory Of Frances Trumbo Jackson, Super Mom
Nepton, Kentucky
Fleming County High School Panther Fan

Tasty Lemon Bars

2 cups sifted all-purpose flour
½ cup confectioners' sugar
1 cup margarine
4 eggs, beaten
2 cups granulated sugar
⅓ cup lemon juice
¼ cup all-purpose flour
½ teaspoon baking powder

Sift together 2 cups flour and confectioners' sugar. Cut in margarine till mixture clings together. Press into a 13 x 9 x 2 baking pan. Bake at 350 degrees for 20 to 25 minutes or until lightly browned. Beat together eggs, granulated sugar, and lemon juice. Sift together the flour and the baking powder. Stir in egg mixture. Pour over baked crust. Bake in preheated oven at 350 degrees for 25 minutes longer. Dust warm with confectioners' sugar.

Kelli Oakley
Lexington, Kentucky
Henry Clay High School Blue Devil Fan
Murray State University Racer Fan

Big Ol' Cookies

2 cups melted butter
2 cups brown sugar
2 cups sugar
4 eggs, beaten
2 teaspoons vanilla
4 cups flour
2 teaspoons soda
2 teaspoons baking powder
1 cup oats
2 cups cornflakes, crushed
2 cups chocolate chips
1 cup raisins
1 cup shredded coconut

Blend melted butter, brown sugar, sugar, eggs and vanilla. Mix and add flour, soda and baking powder. Add remaining ingredients to butter mixture and blend. Bake on ungreased cookie sheet for 12 minutes at 350 degrees. Cookies will spread while baking. Makes 6 dozen large cookies.

Karen Brooks
Lexington, Kentucky
University of Kentucky Wildcat Fan

Easy Texas Sheetcake

Bring to boil:
2 sticks butter
1 cup water
4 tablespoons cocoa

Remove from heat.

Add the following:
2 cups sugar
2 cups flour
⅓ teaspoon salt
½ cup milk with 1 teaspoon soda in it
1 teaspoon vanilla
2 eggs

Beat well. Pour on large cookie sheet. Bake at 350 degrees for 20 minutes.

Frosting:
After cake bakes 15 minutes, start making frosting.

Bring to boil:
1 stick of butter
4 tablespoons cocoa
6 tablespoons milk

Remove from heat and add:
1 box confectioners sugar
1 teaspoon vanilla
1 cup nuts, chopped

Spread on hot cake.

Ida Byrd
Lexington, Kentucky
University of Kentucky Wildcat Fan
Tates Creek High School Commodore Fan

Rocky Road Fudge Brownies

1-19.8 ounce package brownie mix
1 cup chopped pecans
3 cups miniature marshmallows
2-1 ounce squares unsweetened chocolate
⅓ cup milk
½ cup butter or margarine
16-ounce package powdered sugar, sifted
1 teaspoon vanilla extract

Prepare brownie mix according to package directions; stir in pecans. Spoon batter into a greased 13x9x2-inch baking pan. Bake at 350 degrees for 25 minutes. Remove from oven and sprinkle miniature marshmallows over hot brownies.

Combine chocolate, ⅓ cup milk, and butter in a heavy saucepan. Cook over low heat until chocolate and butter melt, stirring often. Remove from heat. Transfer to a medium mixing bowl. Add powdered sugar and vanilla; beat at low speed with an electric mixer until smooth. (If frosting is too stiff for spreading consistency, add milk, one tablespoon at a time, stirring until smooth.) Spread over brownies. Cool in pan on a wire rack and cut into bars. Makes one dozen.

**Dr. Lee Todd, President, University of Kentucky
Lexington, Kentucky
University of Kentucky Wildcat Fan**

Peanut Butter Fudge

2 cups white sugar
⅔ cups milk
1 teaspoon vinegar
1 cup peanut butter
1 cup marshmallow cream
1 teaspoon vanilla

Mix sugar, milk and vinegar. Bring to a boil and cook 6 minutes. Remove from stove and add peanut butter, marshmallow cream and vanilla. Beat and pour into greased 8" or 9" pan. Cut into squares while still warm.

Linda Herrington
Lexington, Kentucky
University of Kentucky Wildcat Fan

Chocolate Peanut Treats

¾ cup graham cracker crumbs, 12-ounce squares
½ cup margarine, melted
2 cups confectioners sugar
½ cup chunky peanut butter
1 cup (6 ounces) semi-sweet chocolate chips

In a bowl, combine cracker crumbs and butter; mix well. Stir in sugar and peanut butter. Press into a greased 8-inch square pan. In a microwave or double boiler, melt the chips and stir until smooth. Spread over peanut butter layer. Chill for 30 minutes. Cut into squares. Chill until firm, about 30 minutes longer. Store in refrigerator.

Josh Oakley
Lexington, Kentucky
University of Kentucky Wildcat Fan
Henry Clay Blue Devil Fan

Chocolate Chip Cheese Ball

8 ounce cream cheese
¾ cup confectionary sugar
¾ cup mini chocolate chips
¾ cup pecan, chopped
½ cup ~~melted real butter~~ *Softened*
2 tablespoons brown sugar
1 tablespoon vanilla

Soften cream cheese. Beat together sugar, butter, brown sugar, and vanilla until smooth. Mix in chocolate chips and ½ cup of pecans. Refrigerate until firm. Shape into ball and roll in remaining pecans. Serve with graham crackers, butter cookies, or pretzels.

Sandy Hilen
Lexington, Kentucky
University of Kentucky Wildcat Fan

When the Kentucky TALEgating authors visit tailgate fans in the parking lots, they are sometimes asked to join in many of the parties and even photos! Above, Kelli Oakley joins Sandy Hilen, Lexington, and her group during a University of Kentucky football game. Hilen is responsible for sharing one of the Oakley's cookbook favorites, the "Chocolate Chip Cheeseball." From left to right were Helen Biddle, Verla Oakes, Oakley, Sandy Hilen, Eva Waters, Brittany Burus, seated left to right, Bob McMenama, Benny Oakes and Bob Hilen.

Scotch Short Bread

2 cups butter
¾ cup sugar
5 cups flour, sifted
1 teaspoon vanilla or 1½ teaspoon almond

Cream together softened butter and sugar. Add flour and flavoring. Mix well. Divide dough into 2 balls. On a lightly floured surface, roll each ball into a ½-inch rectangle. Cut into squares. Cut each square into 2 triangles. Prick triangles with fork and sprinkle with sugar. Bake on ungreased cookie sheet at 300 degrees for 15 to 20 minutes until lightly browned.

Marie M. Brown
Anamosa, Iowa
University of Iowa Hawkeyes Fan

Chocolate Waffle Cookies

1½ cup sugar
1 cup butter or margarine
4 eggs
2 teaspoons vanilla
2 cups flour
½ cup cocoa
½ teaspoon baking powder
Pinch of salt

Cream butter and sugar. Beat in eggs and vanilla. Sift dry ingredients and add to make a stiff batter. Drop rounded spoonfuls on hot waffle iron for 1 to 2 minutes (may need to experiment with a few). Frost with powdered sugar icing.

Marie M. Brown
Anamosa, Iowa
University of Iowa Hawkeye Fan

Big Red Trifle

Brownie mix, large box
2 large Cool Whip tubs
3 small boxes chocolate pudding
3⅓ cups kahlua
1 package Heath bar crumbs
Chocolate syrup

Follow directions accordingly to the brownie mix and bake. Follow directions and mix pudding. Poke holes in brownie while warm and pour liquor over to soak. Crumble brownie. Begin to layer in trifle bowl by first adding cake, Cool Whip, pudding, and Heath crumbles. Top with Cool Whip and chocolate syrup swirls. Cake, Cool Whip , pudding and Heath crumbles. Top with Cool Whip and chocolate syrup swirls. I make this in a trifle bowl and sit this in a big bowl of ice! It's a favorite!

Peggy Graviss
Bowling Green, Kentucky
Western Kentucky University Hilltopper Fan

Natakie Dearing, Peggy Graviss and her granddaughter, Lucy, enjoy an afternoon of tailgating at WKU.

Oven Carmel Corn

**20 cups popcorn, air-popped (1½ cups
    unpopped)
2 cups brown sugar
2 sticks margarine
½ cup sorghum
½ teaspoon salt
1 teaspoon vanilla
½ teaspoon baking soda
1 pinch cream of tarter**

Place popped corn in a large bowl. In medium saucepan, melt margarine; stir in brown sugar, sorghum, salt and cream of tarter. Bring to a boil over low heat, stirring occasionally. Allow to boil about 45 seconds. Stir in vanilla and soda, blending well. Pour over popped corn, stirring to coat thoroughly. Transfer to shallow pans and bake at 250 degrees for one hour, stirring every 15 miutes. Cool and store in an airtight container. Yields 20 cups.

**Sara "Betsy" White
Maysville, Kentucky**

*Chad Brady, left, and Wes Bowling showed their support for the
University of Louisville marching band during the Cardinals win
over West Virginia on November 2, 2006, 44-34.*

Tailgating Kahlua Brownies

⅔ cup butter
3 squares, 3 ounces unsweetened
      chocolate
1½ cups all-purpose flour, sifted
½ teaspoon baking powder
½ teaspoon salt
3 large eggs
2 cups sugar
½ cup, plus 1 tablespoon Kahlua
¾ cup chopped walnuts or pecans

Preheat the oven to 350 degrees. Grease a 9 x 9 inch baking pan. Melt butter and chocolate in double boiler or microwave. Cool slightly. Sift together the flour, baking powder, and salt; set aside. Beat the eggs with the sugar until light. Stir in the chocolate mixture and ½ cup of the Kahlua, then add the flour mixture and blend. Stir in the nuts. Turn the batter into the prepared pan and bake for 30 minutes. When brownies have cooled, brush top with remaining tablespoon of Kahlua.

Kelli Oakley
Lexington, Kentucky
Henry Clay Blue Devil Fan
Murray State University Racer Fan

Banana Pudding

4 cups milk
3 small boxes vanilla instant pudding
8-ounce carton Cool Whip at room
      temperature
8-ounce carton sour cream
Bananas, sliced
Vanilla wafers

Mix milk and pudding. Add sour cream and Cool Whip. Layer with bananas and vanilla wafers.

Marge Poore
Georgetown, Kentucky
Scott County High School Cardinal Fan

Jim's World Famous Oatmeal Cookies

2½ sticks of softened butter (I cup of margarine but butter tastes better)
1½ cups of dark brown sugar (packed firmly)
½ cup sugar
2 large eggs
I teaspoon sugar
½ cup all-purpose flour
I teaspoon baking soda
I teaspoon cinnamon
½ teaspoon of salt (optional, but tastes smoother)
4½ cups old fashioned, un-cooked oats
I bag slivered almonds (12 ounces)
¼ teaspoon allspice
I cup raisins

Pre-heat your oven to 350 degrees. Separate the wet from the dry (sugar is considered a wet ingredient).

Beat butter with mixer until completely smooth, about 5 minutes. Add the 2 eggs and vanilla. Beat this mixture for about 3 minutes then add the white sugar, and beat for another 5 minutes. Then add the brown sugar and beat until completely smooth and all ingredients are incorporated. In another bowl, combine the dry ingredients except the oats and

almonds; add to the wet mixture and stir with a spoon until smooth. Next, add the oatmeal and combine by turning in with a spatula so as not to break or crush the oatmeal grains. (They taste better if you don't break up the grain, plus the texture is better). Turn in the almonds next; it will make the dough a little dry but that's OK. Here you can turn out the dough onto a waxed paper sheet and roll it into a tight roll or tube, about 2 inches around, then put into the fridge. After completely chilled you can remove from the waxed paper and cut the roll into ¼-inch thick round slabs for baking or just put the dough into the fridge to chill. Spoon out onto a cookie sheet or just spoon from the mixer onto an un-greased aluminum foil covered cookie sheet.

Bake the cookies for approximately 13 to 14 minutes. (You need to watch how your oven bakes). I prefer to have the cookie a little dry…. if it is under baked it will fall apart.

Cool for about 2 minutes before removing from the baking sheet. Another variation is to put a scoop of ice cream on a cookie!

Jim Wood
Louisville, Kentucky
University of Louisville Cardinal Fan

Jim's Fruity Angel-Food Trifle

4 cups milk
Two 3.4-ounce packages instant
    sugar-free vanilla pudding mix
1 prepared angel food cake
8-ounce carton frozen low sugar whipped
    topping, thawed
20-ounce pineapple tidbits, drained
15-ounce sliced pears, drained
1 pint strawberries, sliced
4 kiwi fruit, peeled, halved and thinly
    sliced
1 cup fresh or frozen blueberries, thawed

In a mixing bowl, beat milk and pudding mix on low for 2 minutes; set aside. Split cake horizontally into thirds; place one layer in a 5-quart serving bowl that is 9 inches in diameter. Top with a third of the pudding, whipped topping and fruit. Repeat layers twice. Cover and chill for at least 3 hours. Makes 16 to 20 servings. Note: The cake can be cut into large cubes to fit any size bowl.

Jim Blackford
Nicholasville, Kentucky
University of Kentucky Wildcat Fan

Peanut Butter Fudge

½ cup margarine, 1 stick
⅔ cup evaporated milk
3 cups sugar
1 teaspoon vanilla
1 cup peanut butter
17 large marshmallows

Combine margarine, evaporated milk and sugar together in a pot. Heat over medium high heat until boiling, stirring occasionally. Once mixture comes to full boil, stir constantly for 5 minutes. Remove mixture from stove. Add vanilla, peanut butter and marshmallows. Stir until smooth. Pour into a buttered 9 x 11 inch pan. Let cool and cut into squares.

Sonja Gaddie
Georgetown, Kentucky
Scott County High School Cardinal Fan

Pumpkin Pie

8-inch pie shell, unbaked
2 eggs
1 cup ricotta cheese
16-ounce can solid pumpkin
¾ cup brown sugar
⅔ cup evaporated milk
1½ teaspoon pumpkin pie seasoning
1 teaspoon vanilla
½ teaspoon salt

Preheat oven to 375 degrees. Beat eggs lightly. Add ricotta and stir until smooth. Add remaining ingredients and pour in pie shell. Bake 45 minutes or until knife comes out clean.

Linda Gray
Lexington, Kentucky
Henry Clay High School Blue Devil Fan

Italian Cream Cake

1 stick margarine
½ cup vegetable oil
2 cups sugar
5 eggs
2 cups plain flour
1 teaspoon baking soda
1 cup buttermilk
1 teaspoon vanilla
½ cup chopped pecans
1 can flaked coconut

Cream margarine and vegetable oil. Add sugar and beat until smooth. Add egg yolks; beat well. Sift flour with baking soda. Alternate flour and buttermilk; stir in vanilla, coconut, and pecans. Beat egg whites until stiff and fold into mixture. Bake at 350 degrees for 25 minutes in two 9" pans. Frost with cream cheese frosting.

Frosting:
1 package cream cheese
½ stick margarine
1 pound powdered sugar
1 teaspoon sugar
½ cup pecans

Beat softened cream cheese and margarine until smooth. Add sugar and mix well. Add vanilla. Spread between layers and top. Spread chopped nuts over top.

Norma Bruce
Lexington, Kentucky
Bryan Station High School Defender Fan

Peanut Butter Squats

½ cup milk
1 stick butter
2 cups sugar
¾ cup peanut butter
3 cups quick oats (I use closer to
        4 cups - 3 is too thin)

Bring first 3 ingredients to a boil on stovetop or in microwave and boil for 1½ minutes. Remove from heat, stir in peanut butter and oats. Drop by spoonful on wax paper. Note: Have wax paper ready.

Leslie Hughes
Georgetown, Kentucky
Scott County High School Cardinal Fan
University of Kentucky Wildcat Football Fan

Zucchini Bread

2 cups sugar
1 cup oil
3 eggs, beaten
2 cups grated raw zucchini, without peel
3 cups sifted flour
1 teaspoon soda
1 teaspoom salt
3 teaspoons cinnamon
½ cup nuts, optional
3 teaspoons vanilla

Mix together in order given. Bake in a well-greased loaf pan at 350 degrees for 45 to 55 minutes. May make 4 small loaves or a bundt cake pan.

Jeannine Diz
Lexington, Kentucky

Pineapple Coconut Cake

1 box yellow cake mix
20-ounce can crushed pineapple
⅓ cup vegetable oil
1 cup sugar
⅔ cup heavy cream
½ cup margarine
1 cup flaked coconut
½ cup chopped pecans

Preheat oven to 350 degrees. Grease a 13x9x2 pan. Drain pineapple, reserving juice. Measure 1¼ cups reserve juice (add enough water to make enough liquid). In large mixing bowl combine reserved juice, eggs, cake mix, and oil. Beat with mixer on low speed until moistened. Beat on high for 2 minutes, fold in pineapple, pour into prepared pan. Bake for 35 to 40 minutes.

In medium saucepan combine, sugar, cream and butter. Bring to a boil. Boil for 6 minutes or until slightly thickened; remove from heat. Stir in coconut and pecans; spread over cake.

Linda Watkins
Lexington, Kentucky
Bryan Station High School Defender Fan
University of Kentucky Wildcat Fan

Dustin Franatovich, formerly from New Orleans, played a washer's game during a University of Kentucky football game.

S'more Cookie Bars

½ cup margarine or butter
3 cups graham cracker crumbs
6-ounce package semi-sweet chocolate chips
1 cup butterscotch chips
1 cup miniature marshmallows
1 can sweetened condensed milk, low-fat

Preheat oven to 350 degrees. In 13 x 9 pan, combine margarine with crumbs; press to form even layer. Sprinkle with chocolate chips, butterscotch chips, and marshmallows. Pour condensed milk evenly over mixture. Bake 25 minutes or until bubbly. Cool on wire rack and cut into squares when cool.

Peggy Reid
Sandston, Virginia
Virginia Tech University Hokie Fan

Key Lime Pie

1 can sweetened condensed milk
½ cup key lime juice
1 cup heavy cream or whipping cream

Combine sweetened condensed milk and key lime juice in large bowl. In another bowl, beat heavy cream or whipping cream to a stiff peak. Fold into milk mixture. Put into a graham cracker crust and freeze. Let stand 10 minutes before eating.

Linda Watkins
Lexington, Kentucky
Bryan Station High School Defender Fan
University of Kentucky Wildcat Fan

Upside Down German Chocolate Cake

1 cup coconut
1 cup pecans
1 box German chocolate cake mix

Grease and flour a 13x9 pan; put pecans, then coconut in bottom. Mix cake mix according to directions. Spread on top of nuts and coconut.

Cream together:
1 8 oz. cream cheese
1 box of confectionary sugar
1 stick butter

Pour over cake. Bake at 325 degrees for 55 minutes.

Peggy Reid
Sandston, Virginia
Virginia Tech University Hokie Fan

Four-year old Rillo was a loyal Western Kentucky University TAIL-gate fan, according to his owner Stephanie Terry. She says the pit bull loves tailgating and knows where they're going as soon as she puts on her jersey. Terry was a senior social work major from Elizabethtown, KY and said she and her boyfriend, Terry Williams, from Belleview, TN tailgate at most of the WKU home games. Williams was a junior accounting major at the time this photo was taken.

Raisin Cookie

1 cup packed brown sugar
½ cup shortening
1 egg
3 tablespoons water
1½ teaspoons vanilla
1 cup all purpose flour
½ teaspoon baking soda
½ teaspoon salt
1½ cups quick cooking oats
1¾ cups chocolate covered raisins

Preheat oven to 350 degrees. Beat brown sugar, shortening, egg, water and vanilla until light and fluffy. Stir in flour, baking soda, salt, oats, and chocolate covered raisins. Drop dough by teaspoon 2 inches apart onto ungreased pan. Bake about 10 minutes, or until light brown.

Linda Watkins
Lexington, Kentucky
Bryan Station High School Defender Fan
University of Kentucky Wildcat Fan

Sock It to Me Cake

1 box Pillsbury butter cake mix
½ cup sugar
4 eggs
8-ounce carton sour cream
1 cup pecans
2 tablespoons brown sugar
1 tablespoon cinnamon

Combine cake mix, sugar, eggs, sour cream, and pecans. Beat until well mixed. Pour half of batter into a well greased and floured tube pan. Sprinkle with brown sugar and cinnamon. Cover with remaining batter. Bake in a 350-degree oven for one hour. Let cool in pan.

Louise Charles
Lexington, Kentucky
University of Kentucky Wildcat Fan

Chocolate Peanut Squares

1 cup margarine
Six 1-ounce squares semi-sweet
    chocolate
1 cup flake coconut
1½ cup graham cracker crumbs
½ cup chopped unsalted peanuts
Two 8-ounce packages cream cheese,
    softened
1 cup sugar
1 teaspoon vanilla

Microwave ¾ cup margarine and 2 ounces chocolate squares on high for 1 to 2 minutes or until melted. Stir every 30 seconds. Stir in crumbs, coconut, and peanuts. Press into bottom of 13x9 pan, chill 30 minutes. Mix cream cheese, sugar, and vanilla. Spread over crust, chill 30 minutes. Microwave remaining margarine and chocolate squares on high 1 to 2 minutes or until melted, stir every 30 seconds. Spread over cream cheese layer. Chill and cut into squares.

Linda Watkins
Lexington, Kentucky
Bryan Station High School Defender Fan
University of Kentucky Wildcat Fan

Andrew Thomas took time out from passing football during a University of Kentucky football game. Thomas, the son of Ray and Ramissa Thomas, Lexington, said his favorite part of attending a UK football game is playing football before the "real" game begins.

Chocolate Trifle

1 box chocolate fudge cake mix
6 ounces chocolate instant pudding mix
½ cup strong coffee
12 ounce whipped topping, thawed
6 Heath candy bars, crushed

Bake cake according to directions, cool. Prepare pudding and set aside. Crumble cake, reserving ½ cup. Place half of the cake in bottom of trifle dish. Layer with half of the coffee, half of the pudding, half of the whipped topping and half of the crushed candy bars. Repeat layers. Combine remaining crushed candy bars with reserved cake crumbs and sprinkle over top. Refrigerate about 5 hours before serving.

Linda Watkins
Lexington, Kentucky
Bryan Station High School Defender Fan
University of Kentucky Wildcat Fan

Reese Cup Candy

1½ cup peanut butter
2 sticks margarine
1 pound (4¼ cups) powdered sugar
1 teaspoon vanilla
12 ounces chocolate chips or 2 giant
    Hershey bars

Melt peanut butter and margarine. Add powdered sugar and vanilla and mix well. Press into greased 9x13 pan. Melt chocolate chips or bars and pour over peanut butter mixture. Spread evenly. Refrigerate until firm.

Judi Hale
Lexington, Kentucky
Bryan Station High School Defender Fan
University of Kentucky Wildcat Fan

No Bake Candy

1 ½ pound white bark candy coating
2 cups crunchy peanut butter
2 cups unsalted nuts
2 cups Rice Krispies
2 cups Fruit Loops
2 cups colored marshmallows

Melt white bark; add peanut butter and stir well. Add remaining ingredients and mix well. Drop by a spoonful on wax paper. Wait 20 minutes until set; store in covered container.

Barbara Koonz
Lexington, Kentucky
Bryan Station High School Defender Fan

Dieters' Downfall Cookies

¾ stick margarine, melted
1 cup graham cracker crumbs
1 cup chocolate chips
1 cup chopped nuts
1 cup butterscotch chips
1 can coconut
1 can Eaglebrand condensed milk

Put all ingredients in 9 by 13 pan in order given. Bake in 350 degrees oven for 30 minutes. Cool and cut into squares.

Linda Herrington
Lexington, Kentucky
University of Kentucky Wildcat Fan

Cheer-Liters

Punch, Mixers & Sippers

Second Half Spicy Bloody Mary

2 to 5 dried whole chipotle peppers
1 fresh horseradish root, peeled and cut
    into medium-size julienne strips
1 tablespoon celery seed
1 tablespoon black peppercorns
Zest of one lemon or lime
Vodka

Combine chilies, horseradish, celery seed, peppercorns and zest. Pour enough vodka over ingredients to cover them. The more vodka, the milder the heat. Let sit in a cool, dark place for at least one week, shaking it up ever few days. As you use the vodka, pour in plain vodka to replace it. If you started out with a strong batch, you should be able to refill with vodka a few times until it gets too weak. Then start over. Serve as needed!

Jessica Smith
Lexington, Kentucky
West Virginia University Mountaineer Fan

April Kaull, second from left, interviewed Bill and Sandy Rader, West Virginia University Mountaineer fans, during the University of Louisville's 44-34 win over West Virginia on Nov. 2, 2006. Kaull and cameraman Chris Marrs were with the WV media, Morgantown, WV.

Bourbon-Spiked Apple Cider

Two 64-ounce bottles apple cider
2 tablespoons packed dark brown sugar
4 whole cloves
½ cup orange juice
2 tablespoons fresh lemon juice
¼ teaspoon ground allspice
4 cinnamon sticks, broken in half
1 ½ cups bourbon

Mix all ingredients except bourbon in large pot.
Bring to boil over high heat. Reduce heat to medium.
Simmer until reduced to 12 cups, about 30 minutes.
Using a slotted spoon, remove cinnamon and cloves.
Ladle into cups.

Gayle Turner
Georgetown, Kentucky
Scott County High School Cardinal Fan

Homemade Hot Chocolate

1 box powdered milk, 8 quart yield
16-ounce can of Nestle Quik
12-ounce jar of non-dairy creamer
2 cups sugar
6 tablespoons cocoa

Mix all ingredients thoroughly. Store in a sealed container. Mix ⅓ cup of mix with ⅔ cup of hot water and stir…Enjoy!

Janie Rusch
Georgetown, Kentucky
Scott County High School Cardinal Fan

Fruit Tea

1 gallon unsweetened tea
46-ounce can unsweetened pineapple juice
½ gallon lemonade
½ gallon orange juice
½ gallon cranberry juice cocktail
½ gallon apple juice
2 cups sugar
6-ounce package mulling spices
2 liter bottle ginger ale

Stir together first 8 ingredients in a large 5 gallon container. Chill 30 minutes. Stir in ginger ale just before serving. Makes 5 gallons.

Kelli Oakley
Lexington, Kentucky
Henry Clay High School Blue Devil Fan
Murray State University Racer Fan

Students Throw "Game Over" Ringer

When these guys got together on Saturdays for Western Kentucky University football games, not only did they enjoy the grid action, they had their own championship contest going on. Not only the founders, but definitely players of the game, Kal Vencill, Ben Cox and Austin Furlong have all three signed the "Box of Fame" Washer's game for throwing a "game over" ringer. The object of the game is to score 21 by throwing a three-inch metal washer through holes marked from one to five on a two foot by two foot wooden slanted box. However, you can cancel an opponent's score by throwing the washer through the same hole or by getting lucky and throwing the washer over the "game over" bolt located at the top of the board. For those who are accurate enough to ring the bolt, they sign the back of the box. So far, these three are the only ones who have hit "game over." Interviewed during the 2005 homecoming football game, Vencill was a junior civil engineering major from Richmond, KY; Cox was a junior civil

From left to right are Kal Vencill, Ben Cox and Austin Furlong.

engineering major from Hardinsburg, KY and Furlong was a senior recreation major from Nashville, TN.

Wildcat Peppermint Hot Chocolate

12-ounce your favorite prepared hot
   chocolate
1 jigger peppermint schnapps
1 jigger Godiva white chocolate liqueur
Whipped cream
Chocolate covered peppermint swizzle
   stick (optional)

Fill a 16-ounce cup with 12 ounces of prepared hot chocolate. Add 1 jigger of peppermint schnapps and 1 jigger of Godiva white chocolate liqueur. Stir and garnish with Reddi Whip whipped cream and a chocolate covered peppermint swizzle stick.

Linda Winke and Family
Lexington, Kentucky
University of Kentucky Wildcat Fans

When it comes to tailgating, Linda Winke and her friends and family enjoy getting together and exchanging recipes for all kinds of great dishes and drinks! The women in the Winke tailgate group include, from left to right, Linda Winke, Karen Cooper, Joy Weiner and Pam Peace.

Warm Up Hot Chocolate

⅔ cup cocoa
2 ⅔ cups non-fat dry milk
1½ cup powdered sugar
16-ounce non-dairy creamer
10 ½ ounce miniature marshmallows

Combine all ingredients. Add 1 cup of hot water to ⅓ cup of cocoa mix. Mix until well blended. Store remaining dry mix in an airtight container. Makes 28 servings.

Ida Byrd
Lexington, Kentucky
University of Kentucky Wildcat Fan
Tates Creek High School Commodore Fan

Gator Orange Slush Supreme

Two 6-ounce frozen lemonade
6 ounce can frozen orange juice
2 cups sugar
7 cups water
2 cups strong tea, 4 tea bags brewed in
        2 cups water
1 cup whiskey

Mix ingredients and freeze.

Sean Marcum
Louisville, Kentucky
University of Florida Gator Fan

Big Blue Fruit Slush

2 cups sugar
1 cup water
1 15-ounce can crushed pineapple with
    juice
1 large frozen orange juice, thawed
5 bananas, sliced
1 quart fresh or frozen strawberries,
    thawed
1 small marachino cherries, cut in half

Boil sugar and water until sugar is dissolved. Mix all together and freeze until ready to serve. Remove from freezer and allow to melt into a slush.

Kelli Oakley
Lexington, Kentucky
Henry Clay High School Blue Devil Fan
Murray State University Racer Fan

Peach Tea Fizz

7 cups boiling water
12 regular size tea bags
½ cup sugar
6 ounce can frozen Bacardi peach mix,
    thawed and undiluted
1 cup club soda, chilled

Pour boiling water over tea bags. Cover and steep 5 minutes. Remove tea bags, squeezing gently. Stir in sugar and cool. Stir in peach mix and club soda. Pour over fruit-flavored ice cubes.

Frozen lemonade can be substituted.

Sandy Hilen
Lexington, Kentucky
University of Kentucky Wildcat Fan

Lemon Grape Cooler

1½ cups sugar
1 cup lemon juice
1 cup white grape juice
2 tablespoons unsweetened instant tea
Water

In a gallon container, combine the sugar, juices and tea. Add water to measure one gallon. Cover and refrigerate until chilled.

Rebecca Allison
Lexington, Kentucky
University of Kentucky Wildcat Fan

Midori Refresher

1 ounce Midori (melon flavored liqueur)
1 ounce vodka
2 ounces orange juice
Crushed ice
Sliced lemon

Mix first 3 ingredients and pour over crushed ice. Float round lemon slice on top.

Mary Platt Clements
Versailles, Kentucky
University of Kentucky Wildcat Fan

Good friends enjoy a day of tailgating at the University of Kentucky in 2006. Posing for the camera are, from left to right, Rebecca Allison, Ashley Page and Crystal Anderson.

Jump For Joy Juice!

1 small package Kool-Aid lemonade mix
1½ cups sugar
2 quarts water
1½ quarts orange juice
1 lemon
1 orange

Mix lemonade, sugar and water until dissolved. Add orange juice. Cut up lemon and orange into chunks and add to juice. Chill well. Makes 1 gallon.

Allie Leffler
Louisville, Kentucky
Indiana University Hoosier Fan

Party Punch

2-12-ounce cans frozen orange juice
     concentrate
12-ounce can frozen limeade concentrate
12- ounce can frozen lemonade
concentrate
12 - ounce can frozen pineapple juice
     concentrate
5 – 12-ounce cans water
2 quarts Seven-Up
1 jar stemless maraschino cherries,
     drained

Mix all ingredients in a large container. Chill and serve. Makes almost 1½ gallons.

Allie Leffler
Louisville, Kentucky
Indiana University Hoosier Fan

Pina Colada Sherbet

15-ounce can cream of coconut
15 ¼-ounce can of crushed pineapple,
   do not drain
1 cup orange juice
¼ cup light rum

In a blender or food processor, combine all ingredients and blend until nearly smooth. Pour into a 9 x 5 3-inch loaf pan. Cover and freeze several hours or until firm. Break sherbet into pieces and place half at a time, into a blender container. Cover; blend until fluffy. Return mixture to pan; cover and freeze at least 4 hours until firm.

Kelli Oakley
Lexington, Kentucky
Henry Clay High School Blue Devil Fan
Murray State University Racer Fan

Cranberry – Orange Spritzers

1 quart orange juice
2 cups cranberry juice
½ cup sugar
1 cup chilled club soda
8 lime wedges

Combine orange juice and cranberry juice and chill overnight. Pour into wineglasses and top off with a couple tablespoons club soda or mix all together before putting into glasses. Garnish each glass with a lime wedge.

Heidi Maynard
Lexington, Kentucky
University of Kentucky Wildcat Fan

Everybody's Punch

6 cups water
2 ½ cups sugar
46 ounces pineapple juice
Two 12-ounce cans frozen orange juice
12-ounce can lemonade
4 bananas, sliced and mashed
     (more may be added for texture)
Three 2-liter bottles Sprite or 7-Up
     (just before serving)

Bring water to a boil and then add sugar. When sugar is dissolved, pour in large bowl or bucket and add pineapple juice, orange juice, lemonade, and bananas. Add Sprite or 7-Up and serve. If you will not be using the punch immediately, then you may refrigerate or freeze it at this point without adding the Sprite. To add decoration and keep chilled, freeze Spite and maraschino cherries in a ring and add to punch. Serves 75.

Clara "Grammy" Wilson
Lexington, Kentucky
University of Kentucky Wildcat Fan
Lafayette High School Lady General Fan

HASH MARKS

In football, when the ball carrier is either tackled or pushed out of bounds, officials return the ball in bounds to the closest hash mark to where it's spotted. Likewise, for all those talegate chefs who want exact measurements instead of just guessing or "getting close," the following tables should help.

2 Tablespoons	= 1 Fluid Ounce
3 Tablespoons	= 1 ½ Fluid Ounces
¼ Cup	= 2 Fluid Ounces
⅓ Cup	= 2 ½ Fluid Ounces
⅓ Cup + 1 Tablespoon	= 3 Fluid Ounces
⅓ Cup + 2 Tablespoons	= 3 ½ Fluid Ounces
½ Cup	= 4 Fluid Ounces
⅔ Cup	= 5 Fluid Ounces
¾ Cup	= 6 Fluid Ounces
¾ Cup + 2 Tablespoons	= 7 Fluid Ounces
1 Cup	= 8 Fluid Ounces
1 Cup + 2 Tablespoons	= 9 Fluid Ounces
1 ¼ Cups	= 10 Fluid Ounces
1 ⅓ Cups	= 11 Fluid Ounces
1 ½ Cups	= 12 Fluid Ounces
1 ⅔ Cups	= 13 Fluid Ounces
1 ¾ Cups	= 14 Fluid Ounces
1 ¾ Cups + 2 Tablespoons	= 15 Fluid Ounces
2 Cups or 1 Pint	= 16 Fluid Ounces
2 ½ Cups	= 20 Fluid Ounces
3 ¾ Cups	= 1 ½ Pints
4 Cups	= 1 ¾ Pints

Quantities to Serve 100 People:

Coffee	3 pounds
Milk	6 gallons
Tomato Juice	4 #10 Cans
Soup	5 gallons
Hot Dogs	25 pounds
Ham	40 pounds
Beef	40 pounds
Hamburger	30 to 38 pounds
Potatoes	35 pounds
Spaghetti	5 gallons
Baked Beans	5 gallons
Slaw	16 pounds
Bread	10 loaves
Rolls	200
Butter	3 pounds
Potato Salad	3 ½ to 4 gallons
Fruit Salad	20 quarts
Cakes	8
Ice Cream	4 gallons

GAME ROSTER
Announcing the Talegate Team Lineup:

From Elizabeth, Indiana:
Steve Leffler

From Floyds Knob, Indiana:
Chef David Dodd

From Anamosa, Iowa:
Marie M. Brown

From Bowling Green, Kentucky:
Peggy Gravis

From Danville, Kentucky:
Debbie Baker

From Frankfort, Kentucky:
Chef David Walls

From Georgetown, Kentucky:
Linda Bramham
Gloria Casey
Joe Wayne Charles
Patty Cornett
Sonja Gaddie

Sharon Hawkins
Leslie Hughes
Amy McGuire
Dee McIntosh
Nancy Mueller
Marge Poore
Janie Rusch
Gayle Turner
Kim Valdez
Carmen Wallin

From Lexington, Kentucky:
Deborah I. Back
Jordan Baker
Karen Brooks
Norma Bruce
Ida Byrd
Malaby Byrd
Louise "Grannie" Charles
Joe Pat Covington
Judy Cox
Jeannine Diz
Dawn & George Eads
Ann Gaudinier

GAME ROSTER

Linda Gray
Robert Gray
Helen Hague
Judi Hale
Laura Hayes
Robyn Hayes
Linda Herrington
Jerry Hibbard
Sandy Hilen
Wini Humphrey
Sylvia Jackson
Robert Koegel
Barbara Koonz
Holly Lynn
"Granny" Pat Marcum
Walter Marcum
Nikki Martin
Heidi Maynard
Sam Mays
Beth Oakley
Eddie Oakley
Gene Oakley
Jayna Oakley
Josh Oakley
Kelli Oakley

Linda Oakley
Rodney Oakley
Ryan Oakley
Sandra Oppegard
Marilyn Owens
Pete Owens
Matt Skaggs
Jessica C. Smith
Seth Stallard
Dr. Lee Todd
Patsy Todd
Rebecca Tucker
Pat Tuttle
Blanca Mikell Ward
Linda Watkins
Liz Watson
Clema "Brownie" White
Louise Swinford Wieman
Russ Williams
Clara Wilson
Linda Winke & Family

From Louisville, Kentucky:
Nora Bailey
Melinda Hurst

GAME ROSTER

Sean Marcum
Kim Novicki
Jim Wood

From Maysville, Kentucky:
Sara "Betsy" White

From Midway, Kentucky:
Jackie Allen

From Nepton, Kentucky:
Frances Trumbo Jackson

From Nicholasville, Kentucky:
Jim Blackford

From Owensboro, Kentucky:
Jennifer Barlow

From Richmond, Kentucky:
Tom Jones

From Russell Springs, Kentucky:
Shaun Coffey

From Simpsonville, Kentucky:
Wilda Woodyard
Kelly Zimmerman
S.K. Zimmerman

From Versailles, Kentucky:
Mary Platt Clements

From Edinburg, Scotland:
George Cowan

From Sandston, Virginia:
Rebecca Allison
Liz Browning
Peggy Reid

INDEX

Appetizers

Bean Dip 28
Beer Cheese 20
Buffalo Chicken Dip 24
Cardinal Cheese Spread 31
Cardinal Chicken Bites 21
Cheesy Linebacker Dip 27
Corn Hole Sausage Dip 33
Curried Chicken Wings 32
Fiesta Crab Dip 26
Fresh Pineapple Salsa 37
Fruit Dip 34
Goal Post Crunch 19
Homemade Pimento Cheese 23
Hot Artichoke Spread 22
Jerry's Screamin' Jalapeños 27
KISS Sausage Balls 26
Mango and Tangerine Salsa 38
Mango Dip 34
Mexi Bites 35
Mrs. Hilen's Chutney Cream Cheese Spread 18
Nacho Dip 32
Pineapple Pecan Cheese Ball 20
Red-Hot Buffalo Chicken Dip 25

Sausage Stars 36
Scotch Eggs 37
Spiced Pecans 38
Spicy Meatballs 29
Spinach Dip 19
Stuffed Mushrooms Cajun Style 30
Taco Dip 23
Taco Dip 28
Tortilla Roll-ups 18

Beverages

Big Blue Fruit Slush 174
Bourbon-Spiked Apple Cider 169
Cranberry – Orange Spritzers 177
Everybody's Punch 178
Fruit Tea 170
Gator Orange Slush Supreme 173
Homemade Hot Chocolate 170
Jump For Joy Juice! 176
Lemon Grape Cooler 175
Midori Refresher 175
Party Punch 176
Peach Tea Fizz 174
Pina Colada Sherbet 177

Second Half Spicy Bloody Mary 168
Warm Up Hot Chocolate 173
Wildcat Peppermint Hot Chocolate 172

Desserts

Banana Pudding 153
Big Ol' Cookies 145
Big Red Trifle 151
Chocolate Bread Pudding 140
Chocolate Chip Cheese Ball 149
Chocolate Peanut Squares 164
Chocolate Peanut Treats 148
Chocolate Trifle 165
Chocolate Waffle Cookies 150
Dieters' Downfall Cookies 166
Easy Peanut Brittle 136
Easy Texas Sheetcake 146
Fresh Apple Cake with Caramel Glaze 137
Fruit Loaf 139
Italian Cream Cake 158
Jim's Fruity Angel-Food Trifle 156
Jim's World Famous Oatmeal Cookies 154
Key Lime Pie 161
No Bake Candy 166
Oven Carmel Corn 152
Peanut Butter & Chocolate Cheeseball 138
Peanut Butter Fudge 148
Peanut Butter Fudge 157

Peanut Butter Squats 159
Pineapple Coconut Cake 160
Pound Cake 142
Pumpkin Pie 157
Raisin Cookie 163
Reese Cup Candy 165
Rocky Road Fudge Brownies 147
Scotch Short Bread 150
Seven Layer Cookies 143
Shortbread 136
S'more Cookie Bars 161
Sock It to Me Cake 163
Tailgating Kahlua Brownies 153
Tasty Lemon Bars 144
The "Bomb" Coffee Cake 142
Transparent Pie 144
Tray Bake – Peppermint Slice 141
Twinkie Cake 139
Upside Down German Chocolate Cake 162
Zucchini Bread 159

Entrees

All Purpose BBQ Rub 101
Asian Pork Tenderloin 110
Bacon and Eggs Casserole 105
Barbecued Meat Loaf 113
BBQ Asian Short Ribs 102
BBQ Spice Mix 96

Believe It Or Not Pork Chops 104
Breakfast Casserole 102
Cheatin' Chicken 118
Chicken Casserole 101
Chicken Casserole 109
Crab Quiche 112
Dee's Mexican Chicken Casserole 107
Easy Grilled Shrimp 92
Grilled Beef Tenderloin 112
Grilled Orange Pork Tenderloin 117
Hamburger Steaks 106
Hot Brown Casserole 115
Kentucky Hot Brown 103
Leffler Chicken and Dumplings 100
Lemon-Curry Chicken Casserole 108
Mexican Chicken 109
Patsy Todd's Chuck Roast Barbecue 98
Pineapple Ham Kabobs 97
"Put me in, Coach!" Chicken Breasts 114
Reuben Casserole 106
Rotini Skillet Super Bowl Dinner 94
Sausage Pie 104
Scorchin' Chicken Barbecue 99
Shrimp Bake 117
Spicy Shrimp and Pasta Casserole 111
Stuffed Shells 116
Sweet and Spicy Pork Marinade 95
Tortilla Wrap Roll-Up 110
Vegetable Pizza 96
Wildcat Pork Chop Casserole 93

Salads

Bonsai Salad 41
Broccoli Salad 46
"Bulldog" Potato Salad 51
Cardinal Coleslaw 42
Chicken Salad 53
Dee's Tailgating Tater Salad 48
Frozen Salad 55
Grannie Charles' Chicken Salad 40
Granny Odella's Fruit Salad 54
Hilltopper Tater Salad 47
Hot Chicken Salad 55
Hot Potato Salad 50
Marinated Pasta Salad 45
Marinated Vegetable Salad 56
Multi-Layered Salad 49
Old Time Fruit Salad 52
Oriental Salad 58
Orzo Salad 57
Pea Salad 53
Pre-Game 7-Up Salad 41
Shredded Carrot Salad 58
Sunflower Seed Salad 48
Taffy Apple Salad 44
Thai Cucumber Salad 43
Turkey Salad 51
Waldorf Chicken Salad 46
Waldorf Salad 56
Walnut Chicken Salad 42

Sandwiches

All-American Burgers 89
Apricot Turkey Sandwiches 90
Corndog Cornbread 87
Cucumber Chicken Pitas 88
Ham Biscuits 88
Marcum Sideline Sloppy Joes 84
Quick & Easy Barbeque 87
Scorin' Burgers 85
Super Bowl Sandwich Roll-Ups 86

Side Items

Baked Beans Worthy of a Touchdown 120
Best Ever Potatoes 123
Best in the Bluegrass Potato Salad 134
Best in the SEC Barbecue Bean Bake 121
Bourbon Sweet Potatoes with Pineapple
        122
Broccoli Cornbread 132
Cheesy Potatoes 124
Cowboy Beans 133
Garlic and Herb Potatoes 126
Jessie Mac's Squash Casserole 129
Lima Bean Casserole 128
Long Bomb Broccoli Casserole 126
Marinated Asparagus 127

Marinated Vegetables 130
Packet Potatoes 131
Pineapple Casserole 125
Potato Casserole 125
Scalloped Potatoes and Sausage 133
Sweet Potatoes and Nuts 130
Zucchini Casserole 127

Soups

Black Bean Soup 63
Black Bean Soup 76
Cabbage Soup 78
Cardinal Surprise 61
Chili Soup with Cheese 74
Hearty Potato Soup 65
Holly's Chili 62
Home and Heart Bean Soup 73
Jambalya 66
Jim's Football Jambalaya 60
No Fuss Potato Soup 72
Onion Soup 76
Scott County "On Fire" 20 Hour Chili 71
Seth's Tailgate Chili 64
South of the Louisville Border Chowder 70
Southwest Soup 77
Spicy Sausage and Bean Soup 68
Tailgate Chili 69

TAILGATING FAVORITES

TAILGATING FAVORITES

TAILGATING FAVORITES

ABOUT THE AUTHORS...
Jayna Oakley & Kelli Oakley

Born and raised in Lexington, Kentucky, both Kelli and Jayna are sports enthusiasts! Jayna has two brothers (one of whom she introduced to Kelli 22 years ago) and has been around sports all her life. She played on the first girl's high school basketball team at Bryan Station and went on to play softball for the University of Kentucky. She received her bachelor's degree in journalism and has been a sports reporter, editor and public relations director for newspapers, magazines and professional journals. Jayna is presently a regional manager for the Make-A-Wish Foundation® of Kentucky's satellite office in Lexington.

Kelli, also from Lexington, earned her degree in education at Western Kentucky University and is currently an admissions representative for the culinary department at Sullivan University in Lexington. During her work career, Kelli's responsibilities have included catering professional banquet dinners, as well as preparing tailgate food for the sky boxes at Commonwealth Stadium. Kelli is married to Eddie, Jayna's brother. They have two sons, Ryan and Josh.

Order Kentucky TALEgating: Seasons I and II!

If you've enjoyed this second edition of **Kentucky TALEgating II: More Stories with Sauce** and want to add the first edition to your collection, please order:

By Mail:
Make checks or money order payable to Oakley Press and mail to:
Oakley Press
P.O. Box 911031
Lexington, Kentucky 40591-1031

By Phone:
859-433-6495 or 859-494-1027

By E-Mail:
oakleys@oakleypress.net

Please send me:
_____ copies of Kentucky TALEgating: Stories with Sauce at $21.95 each
_____ copies of Kentucky TALEgating II: More Stories with Sauce at $21.95 each

_____ Total Copies x $21.95 = _____
_____ Total Copies x $4 ea. (P&H) = _____ * (See Below)
_____ Total Copies x $1.32 (KY Residents add 6% Sales Tax) = _____
Total Enclosed = $_____

* Postage & Handling charges = $4 for first book and .50 cents for each additional book

SHIP TO:
Name _____

ADDRESS: _____

CITY: _____ STATE: _____ ZIPCODE: _____